MINIATURE GOLF

(*Overleaf*) Putt-Putt® Golf Course, Drayton Plains, Michigan

Castle Park Golf,
Fort Lauderdale, Florida

Sir Goony Golf,
Chadds Ford, Pennsylvania

Sir Goony Golf,
Chattanooga, Tennessee

Stewart Beach Mini Golf, Galveston, Texas

Granny's Gold Rush Golf, Ocean City, Maryland

Jawor's Fun Golf, Roseville, Michigan

Salute to the U.S.A. Miniature Golf, Weirs Beach, New Hampshire

Sir Goony Golf, Chattanooga, Tennessee

3

Jockey's Ridge Miniature Golf, Nags Head, North Carolina

Magic Carpet Golf, Key West, Florida

Old Pro Golf, Ocean City, Maryland

(*Right*) Fairway Golf, St. Paul, Minnesota

Wacky Golf, Myrtle Beach, South Carolina

Sir Goony Golf, Chattanooga, Tennessee

Golden Dragon Golf, North Myrtle Beach, South Carolina

JOHN MARGOLIES'S

MINIATURE
GOLF

WITH COLOR PHOTOGRAPHS
BY JOHN MARGOLIES
AND TEXT BY NINA GARFINKEL
AND MARIA REIDELBACH

ABBEVILLE PRESS · PUBLISHERS · NEW YORK

Route 1 Miniature Golf, Saugus, Massachusetts

(*Right*) **Sir Goony Golf, Chattanooga, Tennessee**

Library of Congress
Cataloging-in-Publication Data

Garfinkel, Nina.
  Miniature golf.

  1. Golf, Miniature—History.
I. Reidelbach, Maria.
II. Title.
GV987.G37 1987   796.352′2   86-28798
ISBN 0-89659-684-2

Editor: Walton Rawls
Designer: Helene Silverman

Copyright © 1987 by Cross River Press, Ltd. All rights reserved under International and Pan-American Copyright Conventions. No part of this book may be reproduced or utilized in any form or by any means, electronic or mechanical, including photocopying, recording, or by any information storage and retrieval system, without permission in writing from the publisher. Inquiries should be addressed to Abbeville Press, Inc., 488 Madison Avenue, New York, N.Y. 10022. Printed and bound in Singapore by Tien Wah Press. First edition.

Contents

- **12** FOREWORD
- **14** MISSING LINKS
- **16** FADS OF THE '20s
- **18** FAIRBAIRN
- **20** DELANOY AND LEDBETTER
- **22** GARNET AND FRIEDA CARTER
- **28** TODAY CHATTANOOGA, TOMORROW THE WORLD
- **32** THE BIGGEST LITTLE GAME IN TOWN
- **40** SOCIETY BALLS
- **44** CAN YOU TOP THIS?
- **46** FAIRWAY FASHIONS
- **54** THE WORLD GOES GOOFY OVER MINIATURE GOLF
- **62** MINIATURE GOLF GETS A BAD REP
- **68** EVERYBODY GETS INTO THE ACT
- **72** THE LAST ROUND
- **74** MINIATURE GOLF IN THE FLAKY FIFTIES
- **82** IN OUR TIME
- **88** WINDMILLS OF THE MIND
- **94** ACKNOWLEDGMENTS

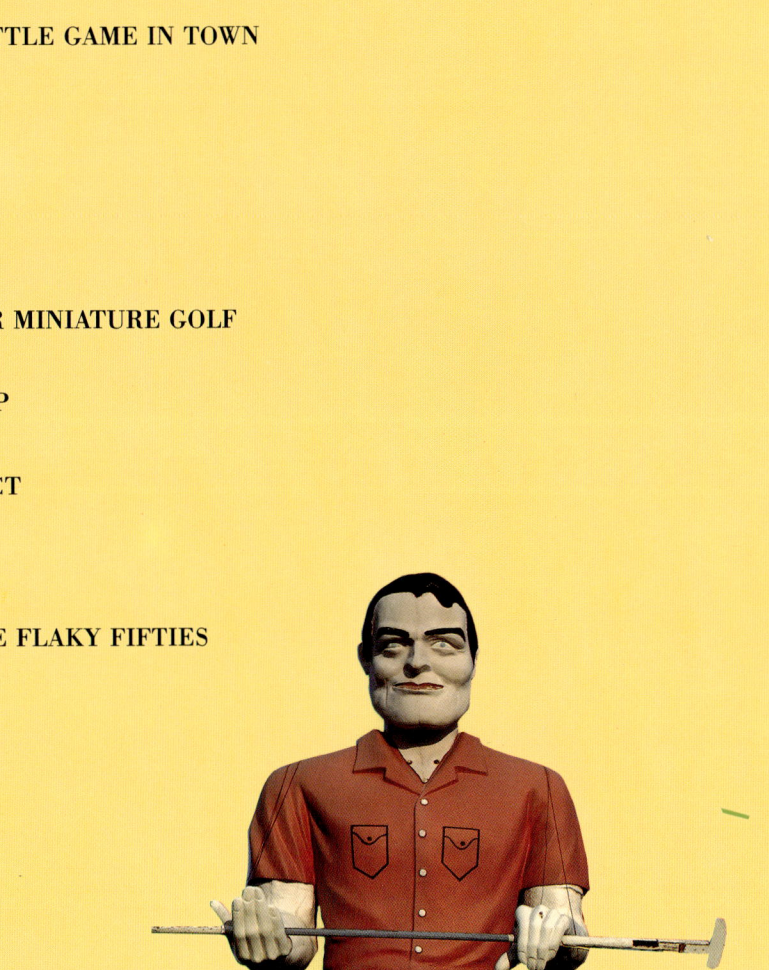

FOREWORD

As a teenager most of my putting was done at a miniature golf course near my house in suburban Connecticut. The course lacked the obligatory windmills and castles, but it did boast one especially difficult hole—the 16th, I believe—where one had to putt across a narrow strip of "green" without having the ball tumble into the open water hazards on both sides. In the last years, this hole was made meaningless by the addition of railings on both sides, making it impossible for the ball to end up in the drink—thereby easing maintenance problems as well as speeding up traffic. My teenage putting was not confined entirely to my local mini-links, however. Miniature golf fever struck me so thoroughly that I designed and maintained my own pitch-and-putt course, carefully burying Campbell soup cans all around the house.

And then golf disappeared from my life for twenty years. In 1978, I began to photograph miniature golf courses, along with my other work of photographing and analyzing commercial architecture and design. My renewed interest in miniature golf was a reassertion of my cultural and esthetic values, and in the past eight years I have documented and played nearly 100 courses of every description in twenty states.

There is a new, complex species of miniature golf, light years removed from the soggy carpets of my youth. The new revolution may have taken place in Myrtle Beach, in the heart of South Carolina's Grand Strand. There, along an automotive strip, nestled amongst the T-shirt places and water slides, can be found about fifty courses.

In miniature golf nothing is sacred. Many of the great icons have been caricatured and pressed into service in these mazes of artificial delight: churches, Buddhas, Easter Island heads, and totem poles. In one California course, the onion-dome church is so large that one could almost attend it rather than play it. It is these new courses in California, located beside the freeways in mini-amusement parks, that are the largest and most complex of all. The statuary and obstacles have increased in size to scream for attention to the motorist passing by at 55 miles per hour.

(*Above and right*) Castle Amusement Park Golf, Riverside, California

Gold mine, Castle Amusement Park Golf, Riverside, California

Castle Amusement Park Golf, Riverside, California

This year, just as I was about to undertake the research for this book, I was very fortunate to find Nina Garfinkel and Maria Reidelbach, who had been intensively probing the history of miniature golf. They astounded me with their knowledge of "The Madness of 1930," and we joined forces on this book project. Windmills had been turning in my mind since the 1950s, but Nina and Maria learned that golf balls had been rolling on little greens since long before I was born. And, knowing what we know now, miniature golf will continue to play its way into our collective consciousness for many years to come.

John Margolies
New York City
October, 1986

Castle Park Golf, Sherman Oaks, California

MISSING LINKS

Miniature golf had its beginnings in 1916, when James Barber of Pinehurst, North Carolina, decided to do what had never been done before: design a postage stamp course incorporating all the elements that made "real" golf such a pleasurable challenge. He hired Edward H. Wiswell, an "amateur architect of fiendish ingenuity," to lay out the course on the grounds of his estate. When Wiswell had finished, Mr. Barber looked upon his creation with satisfaction and pronounced, "This'll do!" From that moment on, the course was known as "Thistle Dhu." However, Mr. Wiswell's abbreviated links remained behind closed gates, forcing the world at large to still search for a thumbnail golf course to call its own.

The history of miniature golf is not the story of one solitary genius working alone but of many inspired men and one truly visionary woman, all of whom responded to the deep-rooted collective yearning in early twentieth-century America for a scaled-down version of the Royal Game of Golf.

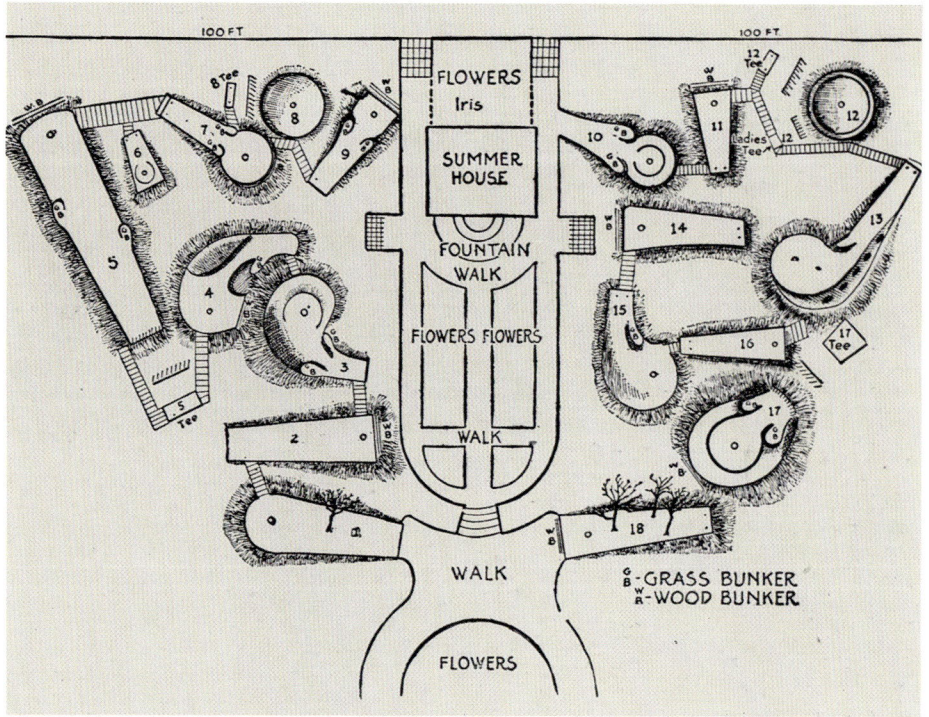

Even though variations on the "big game," like clock golf and English putting greens, had been enjoyed for many years, this plan of Thistle Dhu contains, for the first time, all the elements of true miniature golf. *Country Life,* 1920.

It is easy to see how miniature golf came to be known as garden golf. Thistle Dhu, with its careful landscaping, is a striking prototype of the miniature game's ties to formal gardens. *Country Life,* 1920.

FADS OF THE '20S

The 1920s found Americans dizzy with new prosperity and leisure time, and a pervasive get-rich-quick mentality. In addition to the vote, the suffrage movement gave women social license to pursue activities outside the home that previously were considered unacceptable. Simultaneously, Prohibition displaced many men from their customary barstools. These were some of the factors that created an environment for such new diversions as motor touring, entertainment via radio, and the plethora of wacky fads for which the decade is famous: mah-jongg, dance marathons, Ouija boards, flagpole sitting, and hot-dog-eating contests, to name a few. All this set the stage for what Karal Ann Marling, in *The Colossus of Roads*, has called "the very last of the goofy fads of the twenties"—miniature golf. It is here that our story really gets rolling.

(*Opposite*) A portent of things to come. *Boston Herald*, July 12, 1930.

(*Right*) In the '20s, midget golf was one of the first sports to be played at night. At first, formal evening dress was the uniform of choice.

FAIRBAIRN

In 1922 Thomas McCulloch Fairbairn, a transplanted Englishman who owned a cotton plantation near Tlahualilo, Mexico, became obsessed by the desire to construct a small golf course on his spread. No easy feat in the bone-dry climate, his attempts to recreate the rolling green hills of his homeland failed miserably. Fairbairn even tried the oiled and sanded "greens" then in use in the American Southwest, but he found them much below par. The course was just too coarse.

However, a serendipitous observation by Fairbairn was to chart a new course for vest-pocket golf: a pile of cottonseed hulls near the cotton gin had become a remarkably compact, level surface through the constant tramping of laborers' feet. Wheels started turning in Fairbairn's head. He ground the still-fuzzy hulls, added oil to bind them together, and carefully rolled the mixture onto a sand foundation. He

dyed this "turf" green and, "Ole!," putted away into the blazing Mexican sunset. In 1925, Fairbairn and his two partners, Robert McCart and Albert S. Valdespino, patented this discovery and created Miniature Golf Courses of America, Inc. But they found themselves with a new invention for which no market yet existed. All that was to change in a very short time.

Jungle Lagoon Golf, Myrtle Beach, South Carolina

DELANOY AND LEDBETTER

The only known song published about dwarf golf. COURTESY MILLS MUSIC, NEW YORK CITY, 1930

In 1926 Drake Delanoy and his pal John N. Ledbetter built New York City's first outdoor miniature golf course on the roof of a skyscraper in the financial district. Their aim was to capture the lunch hours of overwrought brokers eager to unwind. Times being what they were, there must have been no end of frazzled financial types to crowd their tar-beach course.

Drake and John also tried a variety of surfacing materials to produce a natural effect, and probably they became aware of cottonseed hulls at golf trade shows, which were frequent events. They went on to experiment with this and finally hit upon a satisfactory putting surface. They claimed to have "stumbled upon" the cottonseed-hull surface, but where in New York City would one come across even a single cottonseed hull? Drake Delanoy's checkered past does little to bolster his credibility: he was arrested one sleepy morning for siphoning gas from a closed service station following a night of intense partying, and, another time, he had his roadster "attached" by the parents of a twenty-year-old aspiring actress with whom he eloped one week after meeting her in Atlantic City.

The height of fashion: Penthouse putters play roof golf atop the Hotel White in New York City. COURTESY UNDERWOOD & UNDERWOOD/ THE BETTMANN ARCHIVE

It came to the attention of Messrs. Fairbairn and McCart that two sharpies from New York were treading on their patented territory, and in 1928 the four men came to an arrangement whereby Delanoy and Ledbetter leased for a cash payment plus royalties the use of the cottonseed-hull surface on all kinds of miniature courses. Delanoy and Ledbetter went on to open 150 rooftop golf courses in the city and to achieve a fair degree of local notoriety. After boasting to the press that they planned to franchise courses in Australia, New Zealand, Italy, and France, they vanished abruptly from the annals of bantam golf history.

GARNET AND FRIEDA CARTER

Although Barber, Fairbairn, Delanoy, and Ledbetter are important players in our story, it is Garnet Carter, a self-effacing Southern entrepreneur and his wife Frieda who are our true stars. Carter was part-owner of the Fairyland Inn, a rambling, elaborately decorated, English-style resort situated on 700 breathtaking acres atop Lookout Mountain, on the border of Georgia and Tennessee. The renowned resort boasted a large pool, ten storybook cottages known as "Mother Goose Village," which Frieda designed, and a real eighteen-hole golf course, which seems to have taken an inordinately long time to construct.

Accounts conflict regarding the birth of the first miniature golf course on the lawn of Fairyland Inn. One account has it that Carter built the little course to occupy regular golfers waiting for the big course to be completed. Another states that Carter devised it to entertain the children of his golfing guests off on the links. The humorist Rube Goldberg suggested that Garnet, having watched his golf balls roll off the top of Lookout Mountain one by one, got the idea for the miniature course while disconsolately watching his last remaining ball thread through the junk pile behind the Inn. A final account maintains it was really Frieda, a designer in her own right, who, in 1926, built the first course solely for her own amusement.

The facts bear this out. If Garnet was the financial foundation of Lookout Mountain, Frieda was its chief designer. She had studied painting since childhood, exhibiting a special delight in drawing houses, and she also displayed an aptitude for mathematics. Her "unorthodox" interests led her grandmother to observe that "if she were a man she would be able to be an architect when she grew up." Garnet valued Frieda's esthetic sensibility highly and encouraged her architectural endeavors. Using a small drafting kit Frieda went on to design numerous houses, garages, and the Fairyland Gas Station, working closely with the contractors. In addition to reinforcing the never-never land atmosphere the Inn strove to create, Frieda saw her "Tom Thumb" course on the front lawn as a way to amuse the "golf widows" whose husbands deserted them for the real links.

It was Frieda's love of fantasy and whimsy that made Garnet's resort into a

"Photo of a model of an 18 hole Tom Thumb miniature golf course showing how it will look on a vacant lot in your city." COURTESY ROCK CITY COLLECTION, LOOKOUT MOUNTAIN, GEORGIA storybook playground for millionaires. Serious golfers who ridiculed the midget links, with hazards constructed of leftover tile, hollow logs, sections of sewer pipe—and enhanced with statues of elves and gnomes—soon found themselves overruled as parents began to crowd their children off the course. But whatever the train of events was, the little links on the front lawn became a major draw. The astute Carter, wasting little time, patented his obstacle-laden course in 1929 under the trade name Tom Thumb Golf.

Chattanoogans Ewing "Slim" Watkins and Pollack "Polly" Boyd were avid golfers and regular patrons of the Fairyland Inn. In fact, Watkins claimed that it was he who prevailed upon Frieda

PHOTO BY CULVER PICTURES, INC.

"Local Boy Makes Good" – The Chattanooga News, August 15, 1930.
COURTESY ROCK CITY COLLECTION

to enlarge the small course to a full eighteen holes. Recognizing opportunity's knock, Slim and Polly went on to build Chattanooga's first public capsule golf course under the name Bob-O-Link Municipal Golf Course Company, to honor their friend Bobby Jones. Jones, a world-renowned amateur, had a weekly radio show and was besieged by fans asking advice on how to play golf's new diminutive version. The first Fairyland course was a natural turf affair that required continual upkeep and quickly became "grassbare." In searching for a durable playing surface, Carter, Watkins, and Boyd began to use processed cottonseed hulls. Through the golf grapevine, this came to the notice of McCart and Fairbairn, and they went on to cut a deal: Carter alone paid Fairbairn, McCart, and Company over $65,000 to use their patented cottonseed-hull surface.

W.S. and A.J. Townsend, owners of National Pipe Products Corporation of Rochester, New York, had become addicted to Tom Thumb Golf while vacationing in Florida. They, too, struck a deal with Carter, and retooled their machinery (which made display valves for gas pumps) into a fantasy factory employing 200 people to build hazards for Tom Thumb courses. A dozen artists were hired to hand-paint the hollow logs, tiny houses, and other itsy-bitsy items. Soon three plants in various parts of the country were turning out Tom Thumbs quicker than you could yell "Fore!" The Brothers Townsend got the rights to sell courses north of the Mason–Dixon Line and east of the Rockies. Carter kept everywhere else — plus $100 on every course the others sold. Soon after, Carter formed the Fairyland Manufacturing Corporation, a holding company under which both Tom Thumb and National Pipe Products were subsumed.

Two guests whiling away a lazy afternoon at the Fairyland Inn on Lookout Mountain. COURTESY ROCK CITY COLLECTION

(**Above**) **Patent drawing for Frieda Carter's Tom Thumb course.** COURTESY ROCK CITY COLLECTION

Although Garnet and Frieda eventually lavished $25–$40,000 on their original course at the Inn, any would-be baby golf mogul could go into the business for $4,500, thanks to Fairyland Manufacturing. By 1930, three thousand people had done just that in the hope of emulating Carter's widely publicized success. By 1931 the Townsends' royalty payments to Carter had amounted to $1,000,000. It was evident that the "Madness of 1930" had, at least for certain shrewd individuals, turned into the "1930 Gold Rush."

**Magic Carpet Golf,
Key West, Florida**

**Peter Pan Miniature Golf,
Austin, Texas**

Wilder and more colorful than Frieda Carter ever imagined, fairy-tale and fantasy themes have withstood the test of time.

**Jawor's Fun Golf,
Roseville, Michigan**

(*Left*) Magic Carpet Golf, Key West, Florida

(*Opposite*) Jawor's Fun Golf, Roseville, Michigan

Old Pro Golf, Rehoboth Beach, Delaware

Circus Circus Mini Golf, Seaside Heights, New Jersey

Royal Oak Miniature Golf, Royal Oak, Michigan

Old Pro Golf, Rehoboth Beach, Delaware

Old Pro Golf, Rehoboth Beach, Delaware

Four Bears Miniature Golf, Utica, Michigan

Sir Goony Golf, Chadds Ford, Pennsylvania

Four Bears Miniature Golf, Utica, Michigan

DANGER
THE INVISIBLE GADZOOKNIK
Is Watching...YOU!
GADZOOKNIK

CIRCUS CIRCUS
MINI GOLF
MAIN ENTRANCE

SIDE SHOW

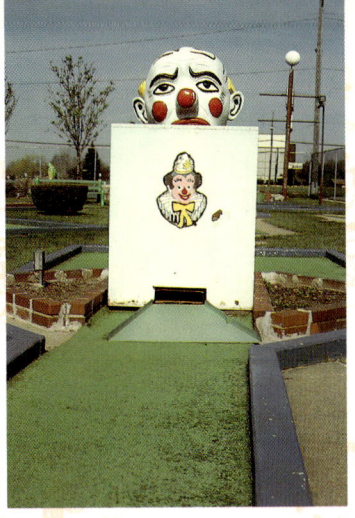

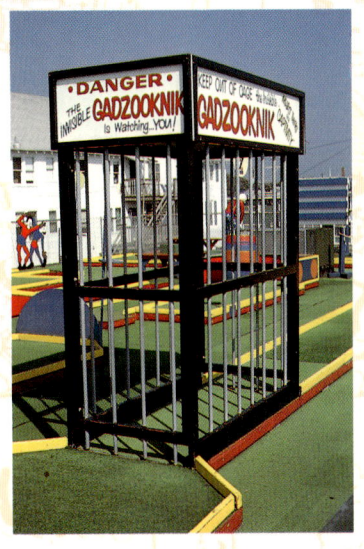

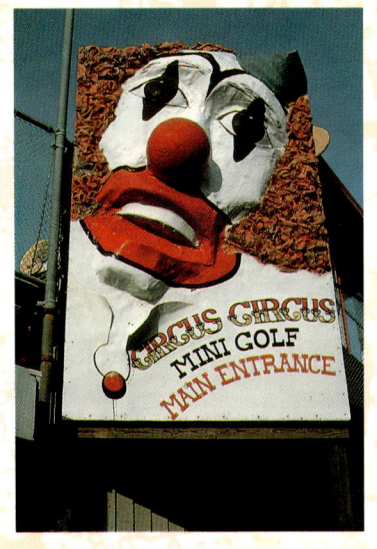

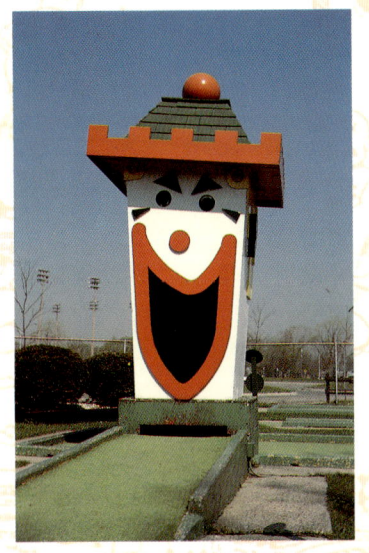

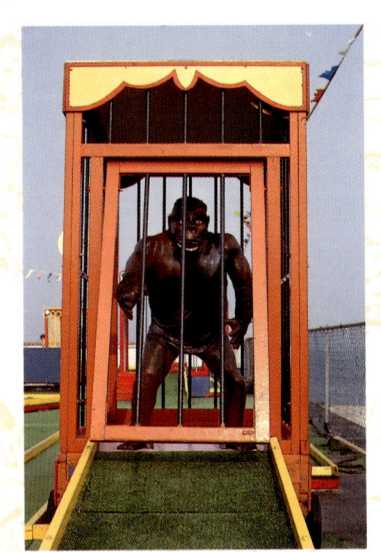

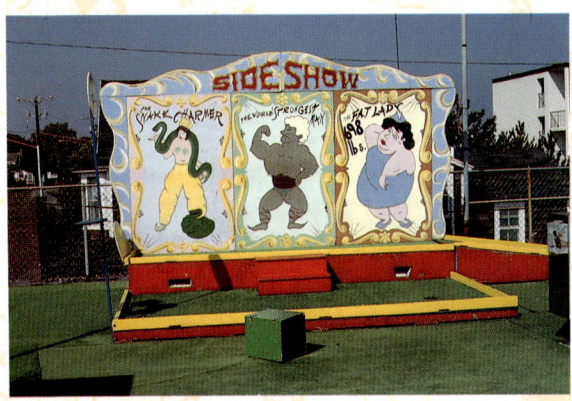

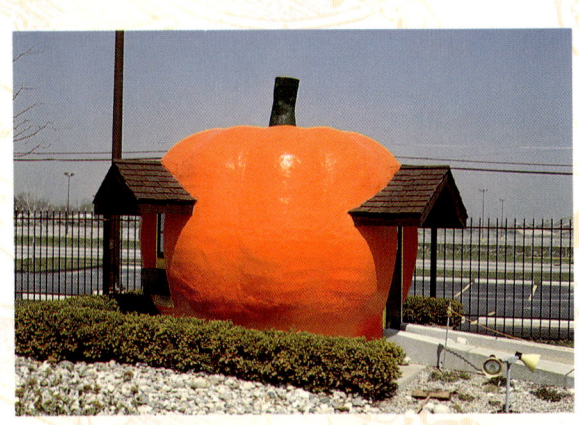

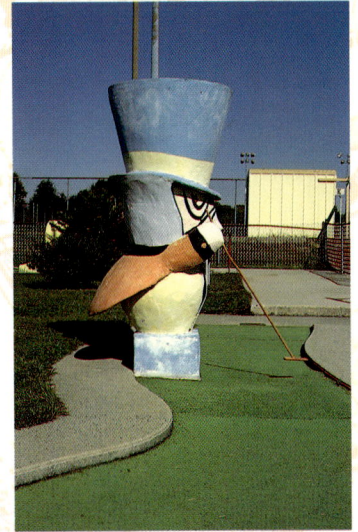

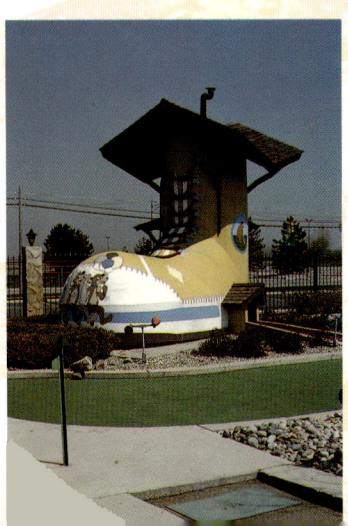

TODAY CHATTANOOGA, TOMORROW THE WORLD

The idea had caught on. Both indoor and outdoor courses strove to simulate a country-club atmosphere, and the results ranged from sublime to absurd. Outdoor courses were landscaped with trees, flowers, shrubs, rockeries, and fountains, with umbrellas, easy chairs, and snack bars to round off the ambiance. Indoor courses required imitation as well as miniaturization and came with their own set of design imperatives: ceilings were to be painted blue, supporting columns disguised as oaks or palms, and walls covered with canvas murals depicting open countryside or famous fairways. Balconies were transformed into clubhouses or verandas, offering drinks, snacks, and room to gamble or play bridge. Some courses even provided caddies.

Although at first an imitation, two-by-four golf had decided advantages over the long game. Like big golf it offered an opportunity for fresh air and exercise, but did not require a pricey wardrobe. Public courses were open to anyone with a quarter or fifty cents, and, insects notwithstanding, demitasse golf was an outdoor sport that could be played at night—along with baseball and football one of the first. It could be played by those who might dream of visiting the exclusive Fairyland Inn except for their socio-economic status (or lack thereof). Others could play an after-dinner round, purchase a combination movie and golfies ticket, or prolong a night at the theater by stopping on the way home to play in evening dress until the wee hours. Ballroom courses allowed one to polish dance steps and golf strokes under the same roof and in the same shoes.

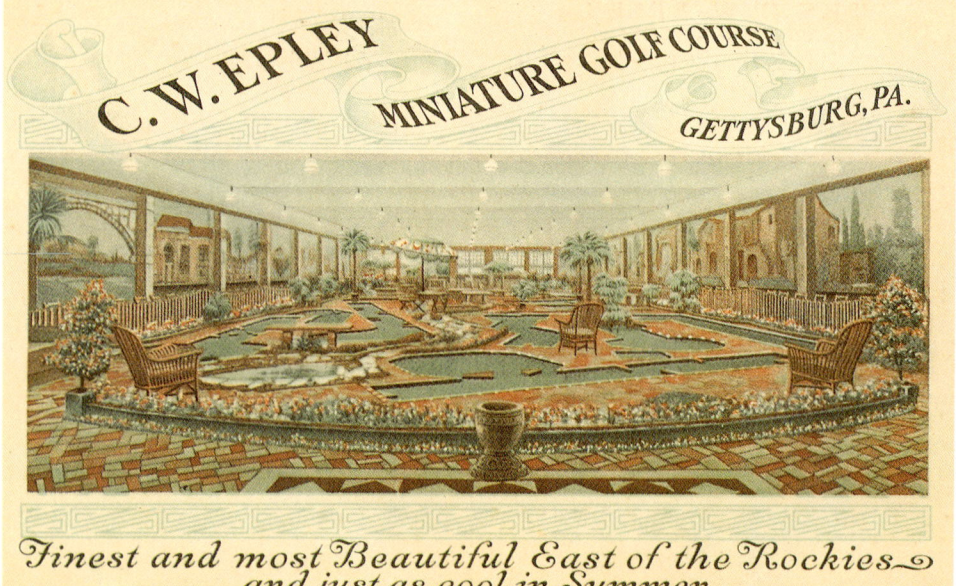

Handsome murals and flower beds decorate a country-club-style course described as a "pleasant way to spend an hour or two in Gettysburg."
COURTESY DON AND NEWLY PREZIOSI

The Crash of 1929, surprisingly, did little to discourage these activities — at least at first. Americans coped with miniaturized incomes by embracing tiny as the ultimate in style. Efficiency apartments, portable radios, small families, tourist cottages, and the compact Austin roadster became the rage. The deepening Depression did nothing but increase the popularity of miniature golf. As Elmer Davis noted, "If we cannot find bread, we are satisfied with circus," and capsule golf was happy to offer an escape into a smaller-than-life fantasy world. The hoopla created by miniature golf in 1930 inevitably brings to mind the question, "Why?" Karal Ann Marling notes that all the fads of the '20s made the participant feel larger than life. For a small fee, two-bits, people demoralized by unemployment could escape into a world over which they towered, masters of all they surveyed. The tiny replicas in pigmy golf brought the world to the feet of people the world had brought to their knees.

An ingenious design showing how one owner brought the great outdoors in. Note the tiny castles, far left and right. Thoughtfully, lawn furniture and ashtrays have been provided. COURTESY HERB SCHOELLKOPF

Around the World in Miniature Golf, Virginia Beach, Virginia

In the words of an unnamed writer for *Commonweal*, "The fascination is extraordinary. It proves beyond the shadow of a legitimate doubt that the trouble with most sports has been the premium they set on endurance, proficiency and the ability to perspire."
COURTESY MARK ROSE

Miami resort guests enjoy pool and putting. *Miami Herald,* c. 1930.

Miniature golf from A to Z, this ingenious typeface is also a plan for playable miniature links. *Miniature Golf Management,* 1930.

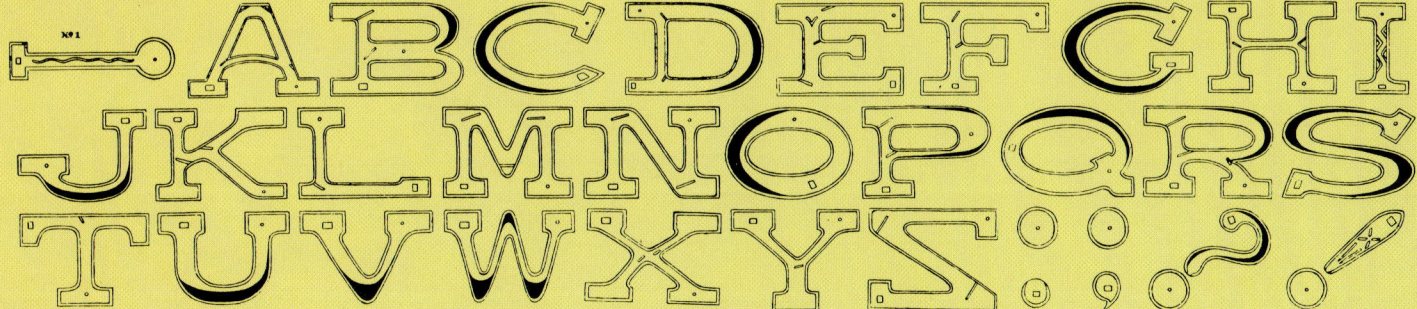

THE BIGGEST LITTLE GAME IN TOWN

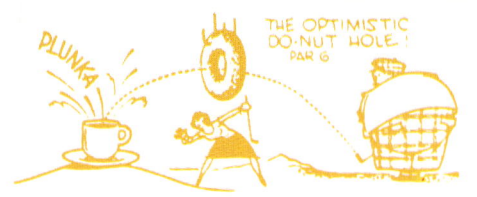

Miniature golf breathed new life into a moribund economy. The craze provided much-needed stimulus to such diverse industries as cotton, lumber, concrete, steel, roofing, and lighting, and saved 100,000 workers from soup kitchens and bread lines. Rock-bottom land values kept corner lots vacant throughout the country. As Will Rogers pointed out, half-pint golf was a good way to fill these lots colorfully and usefully. Main thoroughfares, beach resorts, and residential areas were perfect locations for courses and most likely could be bought, or more generally leased, for a song—especially if that song was "I've Gone Goofy Over Miniature Golf."

In 1930 there were between 25,000 and 50,000 miniature golf courses, representing an investment of $125,000,000 to $325,000,000. An estimated four million Americans, possessed by "The Madness of 1930," were out there on any given balmy night escaping from their own financial worries (and certainly helping to ease those of course owners!). Tom Thumb's success notwithstanding, the vast majority of courses were privately owned Mom-and-Pop affairs, and by 1930 the exploding industry even had its own trade magazine, *Miniature Golf Management*. It dispensed business advice to course owners and breathlessly reported on the latest and most outrageous layouts and hazards.

Runt golf as a deliverance from the Great Depression? *Kankakee News*, Kankakee, Illinois, 1930.

By Thiele, in the Kankakee, Illinois, *News*

THE BOY WHO MADE GOOD

By 1929 regular golfers numbered nearly half of pigmy golf's players; and as golf-o-links gained popularity the issue of its regulation as a sport became important to serious putters. Quirky hazards and trick shots led a sniffy conservative faction to dismiss the sport as "akin to the mechanical side-shows you wander into at Coney Island and Atlantic City." But in mid-1930, even the United States Golf As-

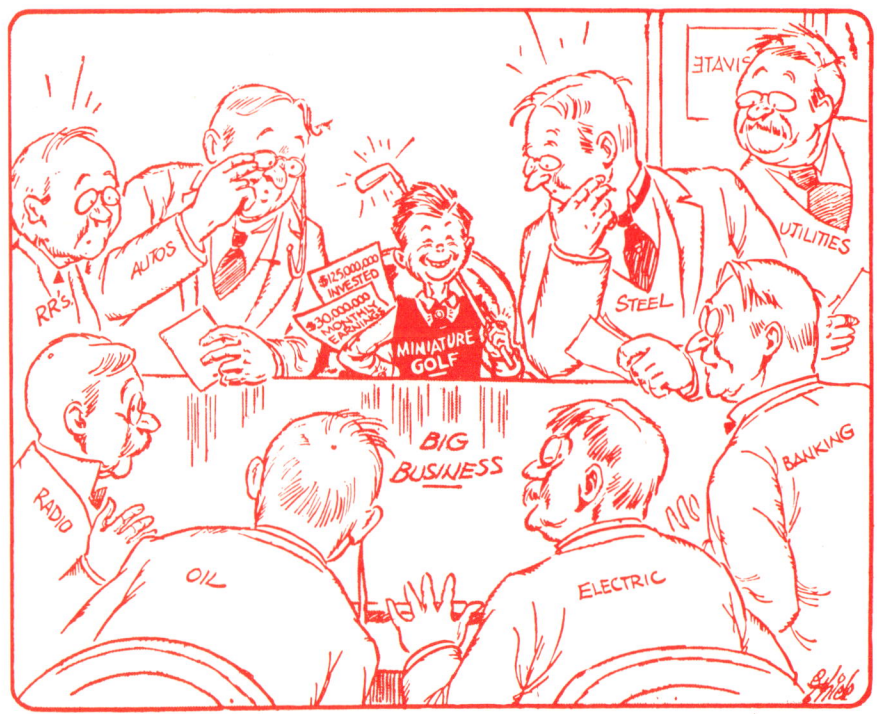

sociation Amateur Status Committee was forced to recognize its stature and issued this decree: "The Association considers Tom Thumb golf courses as coming within the rules of golf and governed by them. Any golfer accepting cash prizes violates his amateur status. Anybody giving lessons for pay becomes a professional." In 1931 the Institute of Golf and Recreation was chartered in Albany, New York, to promote interest in the game and control playing methods. Comprised of builders and manufacturers, its aim was to standardize the courses.

The reaction of the U.S.G.A. served only to fuel the enthusiasm of millions of players. Course owners sponsored inter-course and inter-city competitions, which culminated in major tournaments in Chicago and Chattanooga in the fall of 1930. On Lookout Mountain, the First National Tom Thumb Open was carefully planned and eagerly anticipated for months. A governing committee was formed that included sports writer Grantland Rice and pro golfer Horton Smith. Play-offs were held in all forty-eight states for the $7,500 offered in prize money. Unexpectedly, less than a week before the tournament, the total cash awards were raised to $10,000 and the contest was thrown open to anyone who showed up.

Over 200 players from thirty states arrived for the tournament, including the renowned pros Gene Sarazen and Tom Armour, to compete for the $2,000 top prize. On hand was the diminutive H.T. "Tom Thumb" Barnett, a three-foot-tall cigar salesman, along with the midget Austin roadster, the first portable radios, and other new products celebrating the craze for the dinky, helping to sustain the illusion that the tiny had inherited the earth.

QUEEN OF HEARTS AND KING OF CLUBS

Miniature golf moguls even became targets for the era's gold diggers.
COURTESY ROCK CITY COLLECTION

These holes of skill for the putter range from the ridiculous to the sublime: a view of a skull, the Hawaiian Islands, and a seemingly Noguchi-inspired garden.

Putt-Putt® Golf Course, Drayton Plains, Michigan

Jekyll Island Miniature Golf, Jekyll Island, Georgia

Fountain Valley Miniature Golf, Fountain Valley, California

Jekyll Island Miniature Golf, Jekyll Island, Georgia

Gorilla Country Golf, Atlantic Beach, North Carolina

Old Pro Golf, "Hawaii," Polynesian Course, Ocean City, Maryland

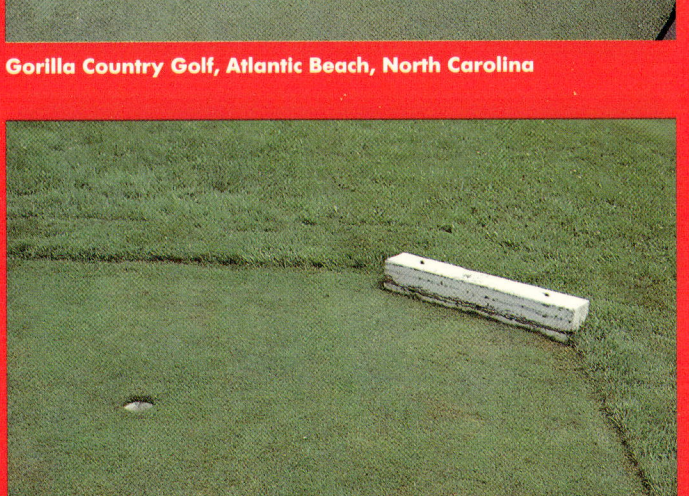

Hutsie Putsie, Deposit, New York

Plantation Falls Legendary Golf, Hilton Head Island, South Carolina

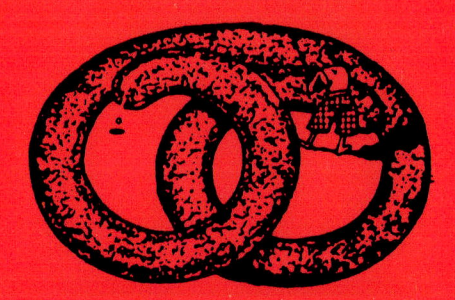

**Funspot Mini-Golf,
Weirs Beach, New Hampshire**

**Jekyll Island Miniature Golf,
Jekyll Island, Georgia**

**Putt-Putt® Golf Course,
Drayton Plains, Michigan**

Theoretically, a hole in one should always be possible, but one look at some of these hazards casts a long shadow of doubt.

(*Opposite*) Old Pro Golf, Rehoboth Beach, Delaware

Salute to the U.S.A. Miniature Golf, Weirs Beach, New Hampshire

Treasure Island Golf, Myrtle Beach, South Carolina

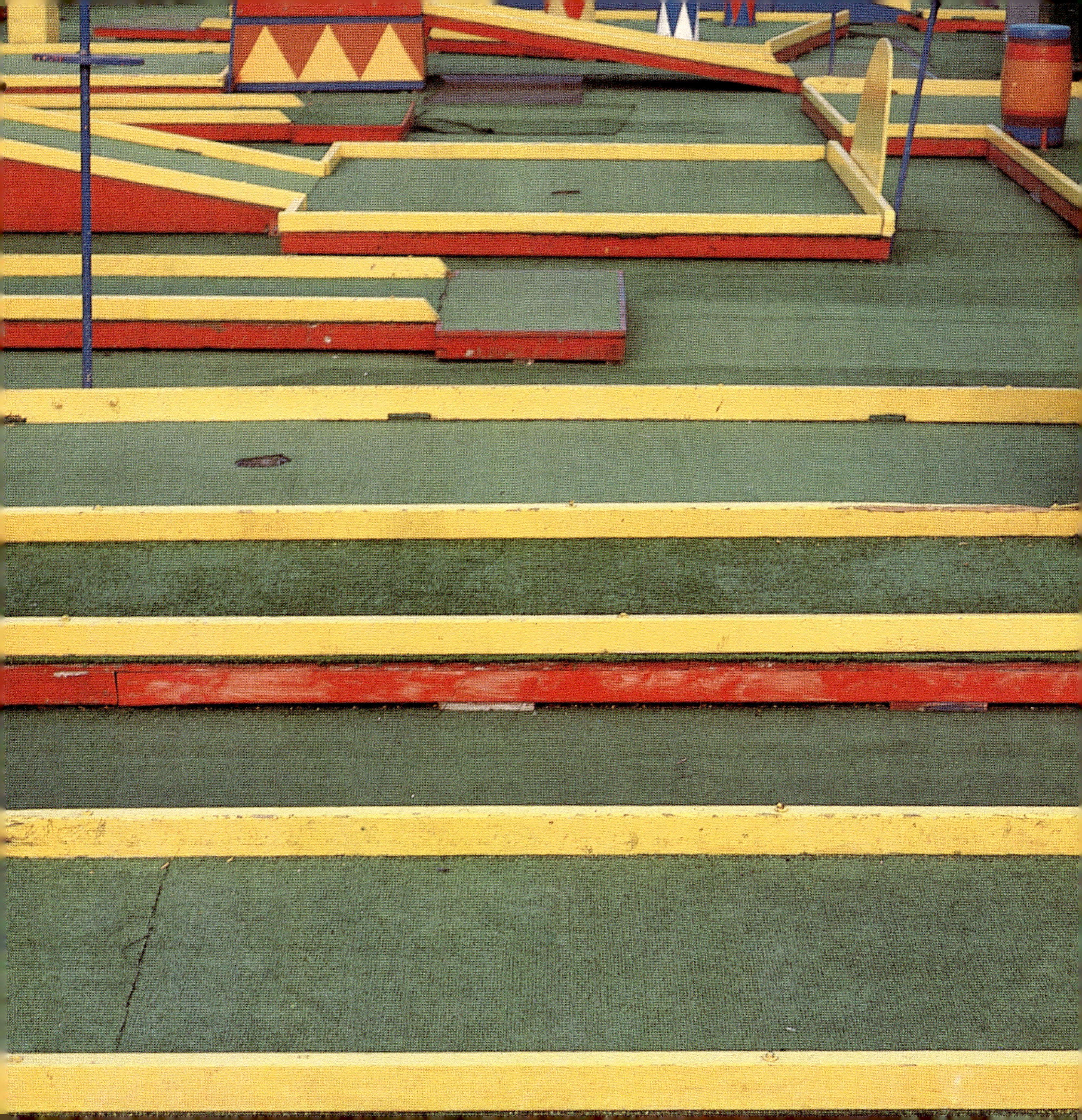

Gimmicks and gadgets continue to stymie putting purists and everyone else. These are the hazards that "big" golfers love to hate.

Magic Carpet Golf, Key West, Florida

(*Left*) Route 1 Miniature Golf, Saugus, Massachusetts

Salute to the U.S.A. Miniature Golf, Weirs Beach, New Hampshire

Hutsie Putsie, Deposit, New York

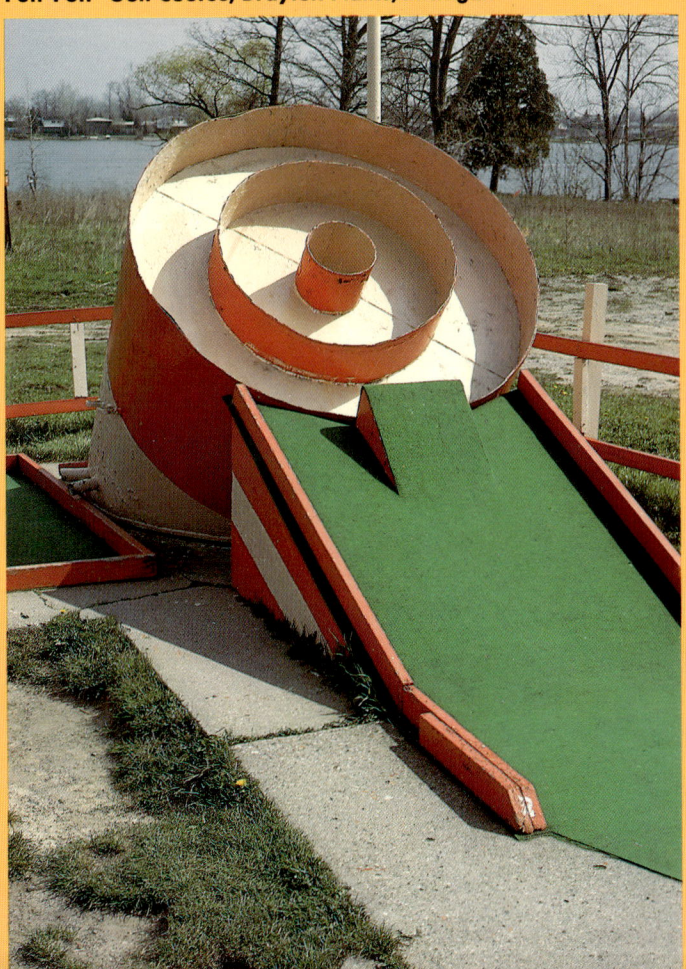

Old Pro Golf, Ocean City, Maryland

Putt-Putt® Golf Course, Drayton Plains, Michigan

Hole in One Miniature Golf, Waldoboro, Maine

SOCIETY BALLS

After The Crash, country-club style courses became a way to maintain the illusion of the "good life." Members of society continued to play with enthusiasm: Sunnylinks, in Palm Springs, was patronized by Vanderbilts and Du Ponts. The Prince of Wales was introduced to the game on the grounds of Laqcken Castle in Brussels and came home an addict, suggesting courses for both the sundeck of the ocean liner *Empress of Britain* and the courtyard of St. James's Palace. President Herbert Hoover's son Allan likewise fell hard for the game, and the Marines were called in to install peewee golf at the presidential summer camp in Maryland.

Highly publicized participation by well-known people made the game even more attractive. Bob Wagner, a Hollywood screenwriter, commented, "Who would have believed that the Royal and Ancient Game of Golf, the sniffiest game of all time, should become epidemic not only with the bourgeoisie, but the proletariat as well?" As the split in society between rich and poor widened, teenie-weenie links became an equalizing element in a stressful time. *The Nation* observed that "when the pseudo-Klieg lights are playing full upon the humble householder from Hackensack, he may not only experience that comfortable country-club feeling superinduced by drooping plus fours and prehistoric posture; he may also be able to capture the illusion that he is John Barrymore at work."

Mary Pickford, with Douglas Fairbanks, opens her Wilshire Links, Los Angeles, traitorously flying in the face of her studio's decree against any involvement with the rival amusement. *Miniature Golf Management*, **October 1, 1930.**

In early 1930, pint-pot golf was universally hailed. Here was a "truly democratic" game that could be played by anyone at any time. Writing in *Collier's*, Grantland Rice described the clientele as consisting of "prominent clubmen, distinguished society women, nightclub habitués, truck drivers, Broadway gamblers, farmers, doctors, lawyers, bankers, bootleggers, Civil War veterans, girls and boys of eight or ten, all ages and both sexes." The public appetite seemed insatiable and courses multiplied.

An interesting aspect of sawed-off golf was that from the outset it was consciously pitched as a sport for which women were seen to be especially well-suited. In 1930, a reporter for *The Los Angeles Times* noted that "putting seems to come natural to most women" and ascribed this to their "hereditary gift of wielding a broom day in and day out," giving them a "keen sense of judgment and touch." Instructors were even advised to tell women players to imagine they were sweeping. The absurd prejudice explicit in such comments was also responsible for the existence of the more invidious "coloreds only" courses, sometimes rigged so that the ball would not roll true.

Miniature mayhem in the drawing room.
Judge, August 24, 1930.

Odd personages still populate miniature golf courses everywhere.

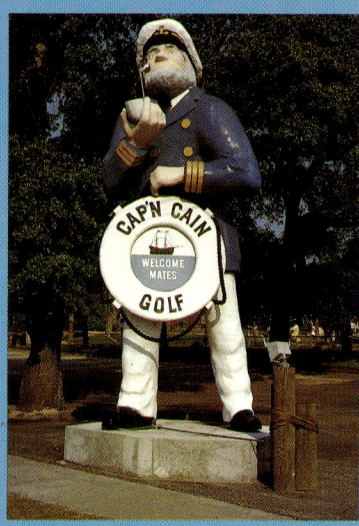

Cap'n Cain Golf, Myrtle Beach, South Carolina

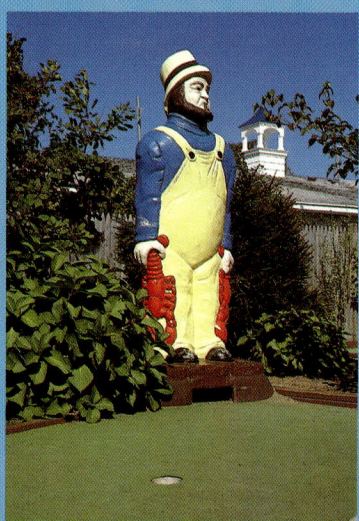

Putter's Paradise, West Yarmouth, Massachusetts

(*Left*) Go-Go Putt Miniature Golf, Hampton Beach, New Hampshire

**Old Pro Golf,
Ocean City, Maryland**

**Jawor's Fun Golf,
Roseville, Michigan**

Jolly Golf, Gatlinburg, Tennessee

**Peter Pan Miniature Golf,
Austin, Texas**

**Old Pro Golf,
Rehoboth Beach, Delaware**

CAN YOU TOP THIS?

With hundreds of courses seeming to appear overnight, competition grew fierce. Then as now gimmickry reigned supreme. Courses began to stay open later, often until four in the morning, only to reopen at six for early-bird rounds. Music became essential, either from a radio or performed live. Grand openings were held for brand-new courses.

Since minny golf was one of the few games women could play unchaperoned, course owners cultivated their trade. Ladies lounges and tearooms were installed and tables were set aside for bridge, also hugely popular at the time. Suppliers urged that "Separate Rest Rooms . . . will actually increase your business!" Manuals advised that it was essential that the courses' obstacles and greens not ruin a lady's stockings nor mar her shoes. One dinky links offered a "'French' luncheon once a week, with a French language instructor in charge."

The development of customer loyalty was crucial. Local beauties were hired to play during the evening to lure male customers, and one Denver proprietor reported a 25 percent jump in business from this approach. Other courses hired good-looking male "Greeters" — pretty boys who were combination instructors, waiters, caddies, traffic-flow regulators, social directors, and masters of ceremony — whose job it was, above all, to move the players quickly through the course so that others could get a chance to drop quarters in the till. It was not unusual for some of the biggest courses to hire publicity agents to churn out stories designed to give their links high visibility.

Stunts were concocted along with the usual tournaments and charity benefit nights. One marathon event in Texas included amateur vaudeville acts and lasted thirty-nine hours. At some courses a sideshow atmosphere prevailed: the public rushed to see Billy Pilgrim, armless and legless,

(Opposite) The towering meets the tiny. A gigantic golf bag as combination roadside lure and caddy house in Jersey City, New Jersey. *Popular Science Monthly*, November 1930.

(Above) The Singer Midgets entertain a capacity crowd at a Tom Thumb in Pasadena. The hut in the background was a standard feature on Garnet Carter's courses. COURTESY ROCK CITY COLLECTION

riding a velocipede and playing a round. The Singer Midgets were another popular draw. Feats of persistence such as marathon dancing, flagpole- and tree-sitting for world records, and eating contests addressed themselves to this same yearning to be better and stronger, to persevere, to overcome all challenges. Owners eagerly sponsored such endurance contests: Edward Sullivan of Olean, New York, was crowned "World's Champion Miniature Golfer" for playing 146 hours straight.

FAIRWAY FASHIONS

The original sedate, country-club style courses attracted both "le monde" and the "hoi polloi," but soon were joined by more extreme flights of fancy. Variations were fueled by Yankee ingenuity and a taste for the exotic; idiosyncratic theme courses and ever-crazier hazards made the ersatz country-club style seem tasteful by comparison. It became apparent that the esthetic future of half-pint golf was to be found not in the straight fairways of mainstream styles like art deco and art moderne but on the dogleg path of the folky, garish, and highly amusing decorative styles of roadside America.

Images from popular culture joined tame, traditional windmills and storybook characters. Mammoth twenty-foot roulette wheels, hounds chasing rabbits, dominoes, dice, and giant checkers provided the most amusing hazards. Jungle courses featured live animals, including a tethered bear at one course and a monkey at another, both trained to grab balls from unlucky putters. Rube Goldbergian hazards designed to put the ball through complicated tricks were wildly popular.

Perhaps the greatest of all 1930s Southern California courses was Caliente in Los Angeles, boasting a pool and sunken gardens. Its "pièce de résistance" was a castle

Present-day "jungle" links have nothing on this 1930 Los Angeles course. The cub was trained with honey-dipped balls to snatch any rolling object coming its way.

"This form of midget insanity has followed naturally in the course of our peewee civilization. Professor Einstein spent his whole life doping out a scientific truth that was founded on space. The professor's time was entirely wasted. There is no more space. All the empty spots have been filled with miniature golf courses." Excerpt and illustration from "Some Call It Golf—But I Call It Midget Insanity," by Rube Goldberg. *Cosmopolitan*, January 1930.

Some call it Golf— but I call it *Midget Insanity*

Illustration by The Author

**"Da-Nite Pioneer Portable Golf Courses"
were touted as compact, changeable, and
economical. They aimed at the hotel,
department store, and steamship trade.**
COURTESY DON AND NEWLY PREZIOSI

built atop a natural geyser that spewed steam some 100 feet into the air. To further enhance the effect, the plume of vapor was brightly illuminated by an array of colored lights.

Coconut Grove in Kansas City, located in an elaborate high-society ballroom, was popular for after-dinner play. Its owner imported mineral-bearing stone to create glistening cliffs and terraces, among which stood both natural and artificial palm trees. In Denver, one indoor course was decorated with "exotic, futuristic" murals, and for the first time neon light tubes were submerged in pools to electrifying effect.

Theme courses provided more complete illusions for escape from the grim realities of life. In Pasadena seven original "mule skinner" wagons set the tone for a Wild West course. In Hewes Park, an L.A. suburb, a "Chinaman's idea of miniature golf" sprang up, with dragons and Chinese junks floating in the water hazards and an "eight piece orchestra of genuine Chinese musicians playing Chinese classical and jazz." Guy Lombardo and his brothers built a musical theme course in New York City using cast-off musical instruments; in fact, the "metalaphone" they used was so cast off that nobody seems to have heard of one since. Altadena, California, boasted the only known links with a Japanese garden motif: it included miniatures of Mount Fuji, bridges, and shrines. A course in Long Beach, California, sponsored Spanish theme parties to complement their mission-style links. If the

In Hollywood, this Eskimo village was replete with blue turf and snowbanks and ice floes and frozen seas. The fan shape depicted the aurora borealis. *Miniature Golf Management*, **October 15, 1930.**

Castle Park Golf, Fort Lauderdale, Florida

Southern California sun was getting too hot, players could cool off on an Arctic theme course, replete with an icicle-covered shipwreck and the aurora borealis rendered in wood lath.

Would-be tourists were invited on a "Scenic Trip through the United States with a Putter," on a patented course. Its hazards were models of

**Castle Park Golf,
Redondo Beach, California**

the popular tourist sights of the day. For a modest admission fee one could see Miami, Hollywood, Mammoth Cave, the Petrified Forest, the Washington Monument, and the (truly) Painted Desert. Owners were delighted that the course was portable.

Miniature replicas of well-known buildings and monuments were Everyman's way of seeing the sights vividly depicted in *Life* and *National Geographic*. One Los Angeles course of the '30s featured a tiny White House (to whose pillars a live bear was inexplicably chained), a minuscule Taj Mahal, and a little Great Wall of China. Tiny knock-offs of vernacular architectural styles such as rural French, Polynesian, and log cabin were found on many links.

By 1930 all those who did not operate under either the Tom Thumb or Bob-O-Link franchise were forced to seek other artificial materials for their putting greens. Fairbairn's patented cottonseed-hull formula was still the best, but patent rights were expensive and the oil used in processing the hulls was murder on shoes. Designers and owners struggled with this problem, and they searched for an artificial turf that was neither too coarse nor smooth but cheap, durable, and easy to maintain. Desperate course owners tried virtually every material possible: compressed feathers, ground sponge mixed with cement, asphalt emulsion, oiled sawdust. Carpet was too expensive to install and hard to maintain. Experimenters in an eastern state were reported to have developed, at a cost of more than $500,000, an odd combination of goat hair and vulcanized rubber. Due to its even texture and durability, goat hair felt became the second most popular covering.

The invention of the scoring table in the fall of 1930 was hailed as a considerable advance in course design. Not only did the tables make the links look classier and more complicated, but, more importantly, they drew players off crowded greens. A major innovation, the "bottomless" 18th hole doubtless surprised some perpetual putters. It not only kept chiselers from playing round after round, but deposited the ball, via an underground pipe, back into the clubhouse.

Golf 'n' Stuff, Ventura, California

Miniature golf courses are an architectural lexicon come to life, from homey New England churches to exotic Japanese pagodas and tropical huts, proving that the melting pot has not gone cold.

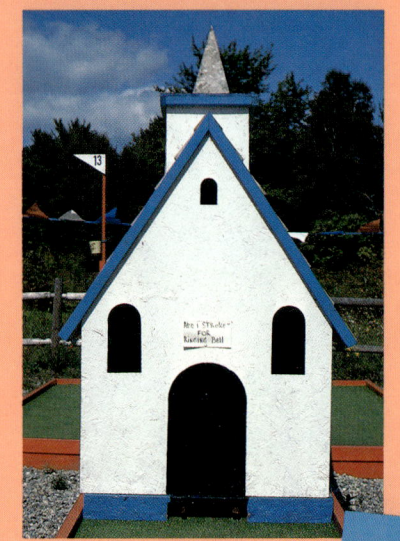

(*Opposite*) Fountain Valley Miniature Golf, Fountain Valley, California

Hole in One Miniature Golf, Waldoboro, Maine

Fountain Valley Miniature Golf, Fountain Valley, California

Rich's Miniature Golf, Wyoming, Pennsylvania

Jolly Golf, Gatlinburg, Tennessee

50

Hutsie Putsie, Deposit, New York

Mystic Railroad Station, Connecticut on the Green Miniature Golf, Hartford, Connecticut

Funspot Mini-Golf, Weirs Beach, New Hampshire

LAKES REGION SUMMER COTTAGE
This model of a summer cottage is typical of those built by "summer people" in the period from around the turn of the century into the thirties. Of an uncertain architectural style, it proved well suited to the needs of the vacationer. Heat when required, came from wood stoves and fireplaces. The outstanding feature was the large porch—a pleasant spot, cooled by breezes off the water—for eatin', sleepin', or "just sittin' 'n' rockin'".

Model by Fred Thompson
Built in 1971

Castle Amusement Park Golf,
Riverside, California

Storybook Land Golf,
San Diego, California

Wacky Golf,
Myrtle Beach, South Carolina

Royal Oak Miniature Golf,
Royal Oak, Michigan

Harper-Metro Miniature Golf,
Mount Clemens, Michigan

Old Pro Golf, Ocean City, Maryland

Rich's Miniature Golf,
Wyoming, Pennsylvania

Valleybrook Miniature Golf,
Chadds Ford, Pennsylvania

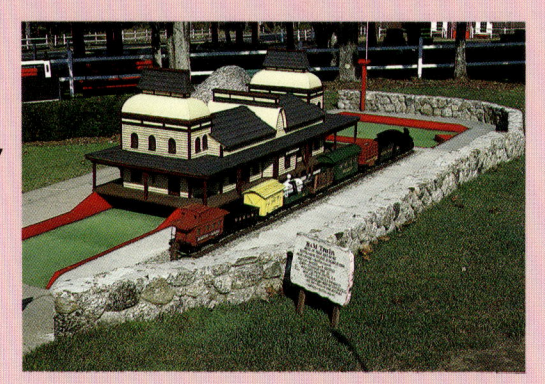

Funspot Mini-Golf,
Weirs Beach,
New Hampshire

THE WORLD GOES GOOFY OVER MINIATURE GOLF

Links continued to pop up in every conceivable (and many inconceivable) places. The Washelli Floral Company in Seattle, Washington, installed a course in an under-utilized greenhouse and decorated it with tropical plants and flowers. One woman in California sued her local zoning board for permission to install a course in a graveyard on her land, incorporating the tombstones as hazards. Prisoners at the New Hampshire State Prison were permitted to build links, and one was also installed at the Lincoln (Nebraska) State Hospital for the Insane. The *Ile de France* became the first ship to install a course with "a net fence . . . preventing the players from driving into the expansive water hazard of the Atlantic." The Dollar liner *President Fillmore* and the Panama Mail liner *El Salvador* followed suit. Even the churches were converted. Poor children built links on empty lots with old pots, egg boxes, doormats, and rainpipes.

"You've never felt the thrill of a cottonseed hull green underfoot. . . . I was a man like yourself once. I had a home, a wife, children. . . . And then I took up miniature golf. . . . I used a slice of swiss cheese for my miniature course at the sanitarium."—MINIATURE GOLF MANAGEMENT, December, 1930

Everybody jumped on the miniature bandwagon. The opening of Caliente drew over 45,000 and was presided over by Los Angeles Mayor John C. Porter; entertainment was supplied by Sal Hoopi and the Hawaiians. When Mary Pickford's course opened, cars four abreast lined up for a mile. Huge searchlights played across the sky while Mary and Douglas Fairbanks challenged all comers. Magazines offered tips on the proper dress: "Summery things mostly, things designed by Fifth Avenue for Southampton and redesigned by Broadway for Washington Heights." Department stores, such as Wanamaker's, designed clothing specifically for the game, including a split skirt for women, and advertised "Tiny Clothes for Tiny Golf."

Self-styled miniature-golf-course architects became local celebrities overnight. *The New York Times Magazine* in August 1930 profiled one as a former "second-assistant caretaker" of the neighborhood tennis court who was suddenly transmogrified into an overbearing pseudo-gentleman with a vision. Typically clad in white flannels and a light blue jacket, he was dedicated to creating the impression that he was the son of a Peer of the Realm who fled England when Labour got into power.

Miniature Golf Management's editor Michael J. Phillips also penned the indispensable companion works, *How to Play Miniature Golf* and *Miniature Golf: A Treatise on the Subject.* The former, a 1930 pamphlet, instructed its readers not only on the

Green dye for those quick touch-ups. As seen in *Miniature Golf Management*, 1930.

Dateline: Ozone Park, New York. Twelve-year-old Julius Hamilton was one of many pipsqueak entrepreneurs who cashed in on the craze by improvising links out of old tires, tin cans, stovepipes, and miscellaneous junk. His "Rinkiedink Golf Course" was ingeniously located in front of a brilliantly illuminated billboard, enabling customers to play at night. COURTESY UNDERWOOD & UNDERWOOD/THE BETTMANN ARCHIVE

fine points of grip and stance, but on the proper mindset of a successful putter. Phillips solemnly intoned that "qualities which make for success in life are brought out on the miniature course. To climb to good position out in the world, one must strive his best and keep his temper; so on the miniature. He mustn't let misfortune cast him down. To win in life . . . or to win at miniature golf . . . one must have a certain quality . . . good, old-fashioned Anglo-Saxon 'guts!'" In the absence of work, the Puritan work ethic was effortlessly transformed into the Puritan play ethic.

Sidney Schoenbrun, a thirteen-year-old boy from Flatbush, became an instant celebrity when his homemade backyard course became all the rage in his Brooklyn community of Midwood. Enterprising young Sid — just the kind of person *How to Play* was talking about — went into business with two of his pals and a foreman at a local construction site. In exchange for bricks and boards, Sid and friends gave the foreman a free pass to their establishment. They invested ninety cents on putters and balls and soon were raking in seven to eight dollars a week by charging neighborhood kids a penny and adults two cents to play on the 8 × 12 foot, four-hole course. Sid's story, along with his picture, appeared in newspapers and magazines across the country: Brooklyn boy makes good.

This short-lived fanzine ascribed the game's popularity to wholesomeness and accessibility. Its editors cite experts who extolled thumbnail golf's capability of stimulating physical development and poise. The magazine offered peewee serial fiction as well, but it did not last long enough to complete even the first story, "Murder on the Ninth." After 56 years this must be the genre's longest-running cliffhanger. COURTESY ROCK CITY COLLECTION

Vest-pocket golf inspired new lines of fashions for both men and women. One magazine described a particularly chic ensemble consisting of a flannel skirt and jacket, soft-brimmed felt or straw hat, and black, tan, and white Cuban-heeled shoes. The nattily attired man sported linen knickers, matching argyle sweater and socks, and tan-and-white shoes, all topped off with a dashing white straw hat. COURTESY ROCK CITY COLLECTION

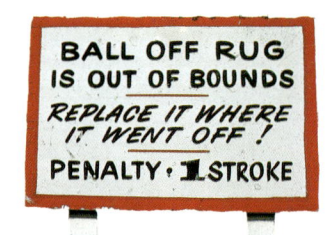

Webb Smith captures the tenor of the times in this cartoon from the *Los Angeles Examiner.... A Paper for People Who Think* **in June 1930. Unfortunately, what Webb found funny others found to be a nuisance, and this cartoon anticipates the serious problems soon to be faced by the industry.** COURTESY ROCK CITY COLLECTION

What would a miniature golf course be without a windmill? Often the central hazard and roadside lure, windmills combine the picturesque with the difficult.

**Funspot Mini-Golf,
Weirs Beach, New Hampshire**

**Buckroe Beach Miniature Golf,
Hampton, Virginia**

Hole in One Miniature Golf, Waldoboro, Maine

**Adventure Golf,
Pigeon Forge, Tennessee**

**Jackson Golf World,
Jackson, Mississippi**

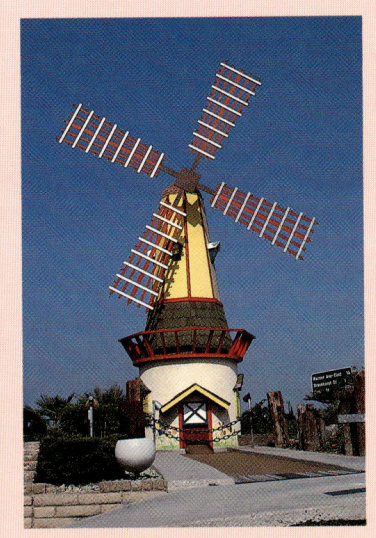

**Fountain Valley Miniature Golf,
Fountain Valley, California**

**Jekyll Island Miniature Golf,
Jekyll Island, Georgia**

**Route 1 Miniature Golf,
Saugus, Massachusetts**

**Jawor's Fun Golf,
Roseville, Michigan**

Sir Goony Golf, Chattanooga, Tennessee

59

A close runner-up in popularity to the windmill is the lighthouse, which is possibly even more romantic.

**Pelican Point Miniature Golf,
North Myrtle Beach, South Carolina**

**Ocean Mini-Golf,
Kill Devil Hills, North Carolina**

**Salute to the U.S.A. Miniature Golf,
Weirs Beach, New Hampshire**

**Route 1 Miniature Golf,
Saugus, Massachusetts**

**Forbes Carpet Golf,
Nags Head, North Carolina**

**Cap'n Cain Golf,
Myrtle Beach, South Carolina**

60

Lighthouse Golf, Emerald Isle, North Carolina

Putter's Paradise Miniature Golf, West Yarmouth, Massachusetts

Rich's Miniature Golf, Wyoming, Pennsylvania

MINIATURE GOLF GETS A BAD REP

All was not fun and games in the land of tiny windmills and cutesy castles. A blessing for many, bootleg golf was also a curse to a few: the putter clearly swung both ways. Some saw the game as an effective crime deterrent since its popularity forced many pool halls, commonly held to be dens of iniquity, to rack their cue sticks permanently. Others saw the courses as just iniquitous dens in the making. Some were glad to see vacant lots turned into garden spots, since they were eyesores and dismal reminders of the state of the union. Others were up in arms over the racket caused by the putting hordes. A large number of the estimated four million players liked to putt until dawn's early light, keeping those living nearby awake with rounds of expletives bellowed over missed shots.

Across the country ordinances were enacted and curfews instituted to bring some semblance of sanity to communities driven crazy by "The Madness of 1930." Wily course owners tried all sorts of ploys to get around curfews: one California operator took advantage of a loophole that forced him to close at midnight by reopening fifteen minutes later. The National Association of Golf Course Owners hired high-powered lawyers to fight the early closing laws. The Tom Thumb Association voluntarily agreed to close its links at 1:00 A.M. but vowed to fight the law. In New York City, 200,000 signatures were collected on a petition to repeal the anti-Lilliput legislation.

In addition to curfews, communities invoked Blue Laws to try to prohibit Sunday play. Ingenious operators devised ways to get around those also. In Victoria, British Columbia, several courses operated under the guise of a country club with registered "members" to circumvent the local ban, while in East Orange, New Jersey, an unprecedented thousand citizens turned out for a town council debate on night and Sunday play. Alas, the pro-pony golf faction lost—but narrowly.

Debates raged about zoning and license fees, which suddenly became germane when previously empty lots attracted several thousand quarters every week. Prominent residents of Ontario, California, feared that pocket-edition golf courses operat-

The Rocky Mountain News, Denver, May 1930. COURTESY ROCK CITY COLLECTION ing in residential areas would create dangerous zoning precedents and "open the way for filling stations." They were unwilling to foresee that roadside America was going to pave its way past their front door no matter how many legislative roadblocks were erected.

Ugly rumors of Mob involvement in the game surfaced in big cities such as New York, where it was reported that course owners were regularly forced to cough up $25 protection money. The '30s would not have been the '30s without Al Capone, and neither, apparently, would tabloid golf — at least according to some particularly perspicacious Capone watchers. Stories such as "New Drive to Break Chicago Gang Rule / Toy Golf Latest Racket" told of gangster tactics to "organize" Chicago's 300

Lilliput links like this one in a residential section of Chicago came to be seen as contributing to the corruption of youth and as almost the equivalent of pool halls.
COURTESY UNDERWOOD & UNDERWOOD/THE BETTMANN ARCHIVE

(*Opposite*) Headlines like "Shouts Keep Baby Awake" often heralded front-page news in the summer of 1930 as half-pint golf's popularity reached its zenith. The *New York Times* alone published more than 40 articles on the Big Apple's battle with little golf.

courses and exact $35 "initiation fees" plus monthly "dues" of five bucks. The truth of these charges is questionable, and, in light of the fact that the game's bubble was about to burst, miniature golf would not have been a good bet for heavy, long-term racketeering.

In 1930 *American City* magazine wrote: "Miniature golf can indisputably lay claim to having inspired more legislation and called into play more existing legislation in a few months than any other form of entertainment on record."

Not only was night play a problem, but many took offense at Sunday play as well. One New Jersey councilman ruled that local courses could operate on Sunday as long as the community at large went along, stating: "People who live near the church are forced to listen to weekly choir practice, now let the church be annoyed a little by duffers!" COURTESY ROCK CITY COLLECTION

Appearing first in 1930, castles quickly became a fixture on many links. The styles range from huge fairy-tale confections to more playful, smaller efforts.

Castle Park Golf, Fort Lauderdale, Florida

Magic Carpet Golf, Key West, Florida

Pomona Valley Golf, Upland, California

Peter Pan Miniature Golf, Austin, Texas

65

Fountain Valley Miniature Golf, Fountain Valley, California

Nags Head, North Carolina

Harper-Metro Miniature Golf, Mount Clemens, Michigan

Sir Goony Golf, Chattanooga, Tennessee

Valleybrook Miniature Golf, Chadds Ford, Pennsylvania

Jackson Golf World, Jackson, Mississippi

EVERYBODY GETS INTO THE ACT

Although one 1930 headline proclaimed, "Miniature Golf Helps Many Kinds of Business," there was one very big business that did not profit from the boom. The movie industry took a major drubbing as crowds flocked to the courses instead of the flicks. *The New York Times* noted that garden golf "gave some indication of replacing movies as the nation's fifth largest industry." The paper even went on to suggest that "musicians thrown out of work by the mechanical talkies . . . might find work on links as caddies in the pleasantly familiar atmosphere" of theaters recently reincarnated as indoor miniatures. With box office receipts plummeting as much as 25 percent during the game's heyday, owners of darkened theaters and industry big shots became increasingly aggressive. Film producers

Fred Astaire stepping out to play golfies atop the Hotel White. Too bad the studios discouraged their stars from being seen on the links; the world can only imagine what a Fred and Ginger miniature golf extravaganza could have been like.

(**Opposite**) **Here we see Fay Wray sans King Kong enjoying a round at one of the more elegant of the 300-plus courses in Hollywood.** BOTH COURTESY UNDERWOOD & UNDERWOOD/THE BETTMANN ARCHIVE

68

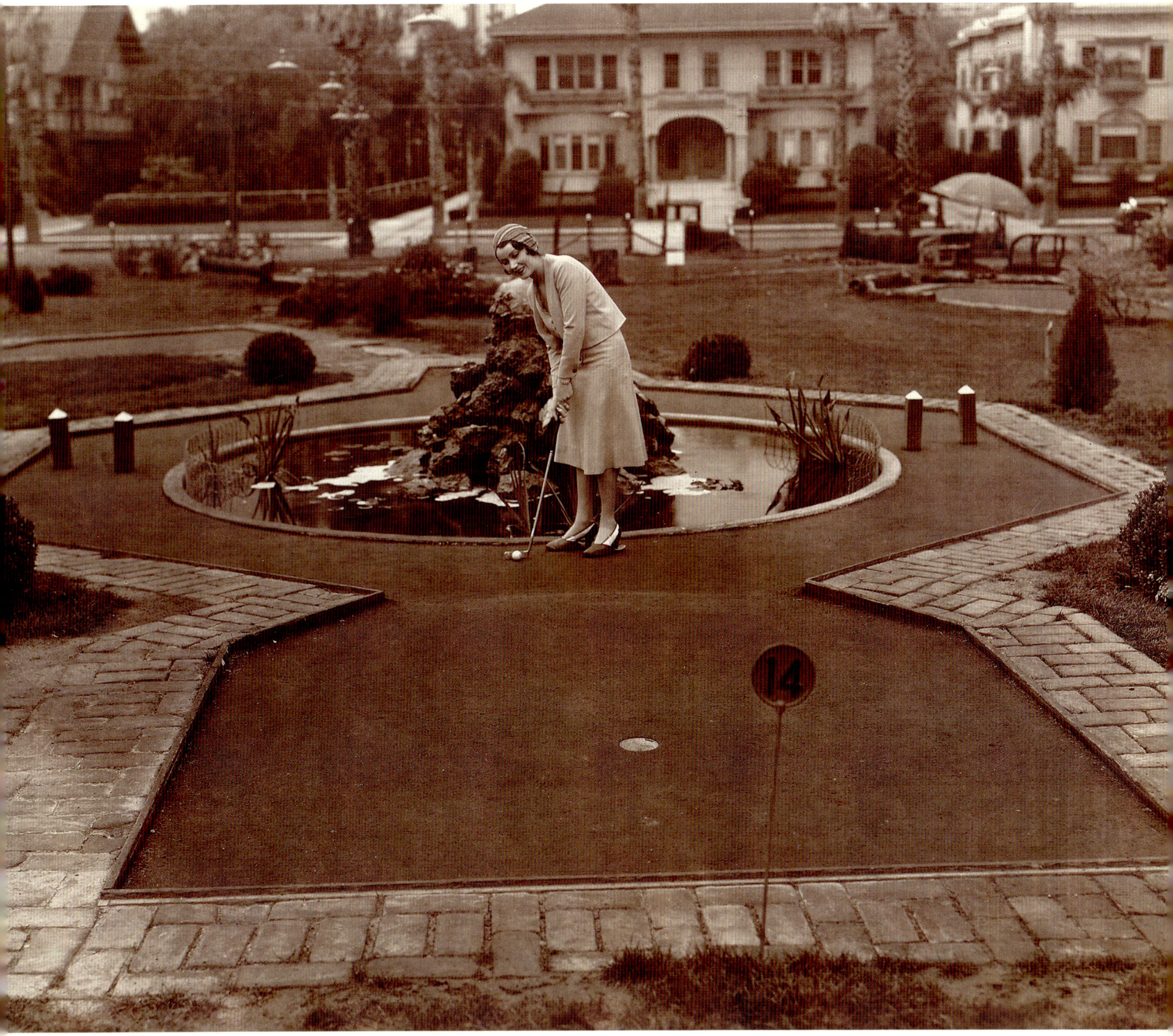
14

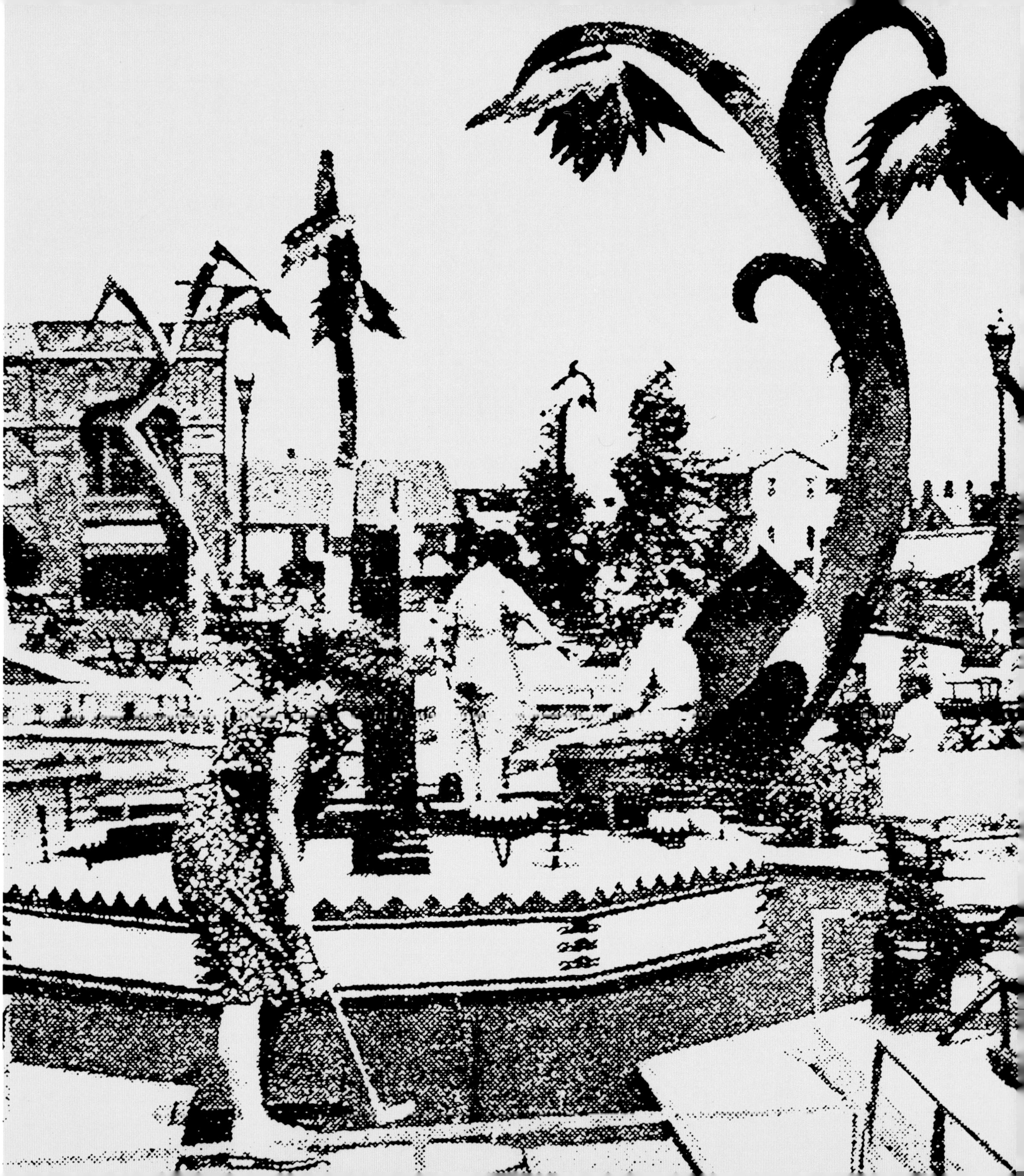

ordered stars to stay off the links. One unnamed executive told a reporter that he'd received orders from his superiors "to in no way cooperate with miniature golf courses. Our policy towards them is to be complete indifference."

Such edicts seemed to have little effect on Mary Pickford, who built her own, surreal, Max Ernst–inspired course. Jackie Coogan also bit the hand that fed him and built his own private links — although gossip columnists had it that he was such a lonely guy he ended up playing the public courses just to have company. Apparently the studios had no better success with Ruth Roland, Fay Wray, Charles Farrell, and the everlovely Fifi d'Orsay, who saw their local links as prime backdrops for sure-to-be-published "candid photos."

Eventually such biggies as Fox Theaters, Warner Brothers, and Famous Players decided to join 'em since they couldn't beat 'em. They announced plans to build courses and convert unprofitable theaters into "country clubs." H.B. Franklin, a Fox executive, explained their decision by stating that "we of the theaters are in the entertainment business. When thousands upon thousands of people decide almost overnight that miniature golf is entertainment, then we must pay attention."

Built in the "modernistic French style," Mary Pickford's course boasted a lily pond that featured underwater illumination. The surrealistic palms were lights in disguise.
Modern Mechanics and Inventions,
January 1931.

THE LAST ROUND

Even though the winter of 1930–31 saw miniature golf move indoors to hotels, stores, clubs, and even bowling alleys where links replaced lanes, it would soon become sadly evident that the game was on the wane. Encouraged by strangling legal restrictions and pimple golf's increasingly poor reputation, opponents saw an easy prey.

One columnist, who saw it as contributing to the unemployment problem, went so far as to castigate President Hoover for not "lifting a finger to cure the country" of the midget insanity and for failing to prevent corner lots from turning into "booby-hatches." Even Will Rogers turned against the game, declaring "there is millions got a 'putter' in their hand when they ought to have a shovel. Half of America is bent over. In two more generations our children will grow upwards as far as the hips, then they will turn off at right angles, and with their arms hanging down we will be right back where we started from. Darwin was right." Baseball managers lost boys to jobs as caddies and worried about preemie golf becoming the new national sport.

As early as January 1931 the handwriting was on the wall. Although Fairyland Manufacturing reported a pre-tax income of $211,519 for the first nine months of 1930, in October, the month of the biggest little golf tournament ever (which Garnet Carter sponsored), Tom Thumb was sold for $200,000 to W.H. Robinson, an H.J. Heinz pickle manufacturer from Philadelphia. "Before going into the deal, however, [Robinson] asked me if there wasn't some kind of trick to it. I told him there must be, but I couldn't find it," Carter remarked at the time of the sale, in his best aw-shucks manner.

At the time of his sale of the Tom Thumb company, Garnet Carter told a Chattanooga newspaper, "I haven't any children, but I have the finest collie dog you ever saw. I'm crazy about my wife and dog and most everybody else. In fact, I think this is a wonderful world to live in – and who wouldn't if they had stumbled upon a darn fool piece of luck like I did." He sure wasn't whistling Dixie. COURTESY ROCK CITY COLLECTION

72

The sale of Tom Thumb came as a shock and was Big News. Why would Carter want to sell such a proven money-maker? But being a seasoned businessman he knew the value of the axiom "quit while you're ahead," and apparently did just that. Shortly after its purchase by Robinson, Tom Thumb went public. By late 1931 interest in the game had nearly evaporated, and courses were closing with the same rapidity with which they opened just one short year ago. As the editor of *Miniature Golf Management* put it: "Every course that opens from now on is just one more too many," or as a reader of the magazine wrote in, "The public is being putted to death." Indeed, miniature golf itself seemed to disappear like a ball down the 18th hole. It was the end of an era.

The Vanishing American.

By the summer of 1931, most miniature golf courses lay abandoned, victims of legal restrictions, burdensome license fees and taxes, a worsening economy, and market saturation. For previously passionate putters the thrill was gone. *Life*, **July 1931.**
COURTESY ROCK CITY COLLECTION

(*Left*) **Brigantine Castle Pier, Brigantine, New Jersey**

73

MINIATURE GOLF IN THE FLAKY FIFTIES

For many of us, our images of miniature golf were formed on the courses of the '50s. Mentioning miniature golf to just about anyone will produce a faraway look as childhood memories come flooding back—memories of soft, dreamy midsummer evenings that stayed light until late, memories of a time when time itself seemed to melt away in the endless expanse of summer.

The baby boom and growth of suburbia in postwar America played midwife to the rebirth of baby golf in the 1950s. The new courses were located mainly in the shopping strips that defined the suburban landscape. Land in the newly parsed subdivisions was plentiful, reasonably priced, and increasingly accessible as "Ike's autobahns" and expressways began to connect the dots and link the country's innumerable Levittowns. Rather than a mania, sample-size golf became a quiet way to spend a Saturday afternoon with the kids or an evening with a date. Miniature golf was above all a clean, wholesome family activity and an enhancement rather than a bane to the community.

The new breed of pony-golf-course owners saw themselves as proprietors of "sound sports entertainment enterprises." Operators' manuals of the period stressed professionalism, sound business strategies, and standardization. Many hazards were echoes of the earlier period: barrels, storybook characters, and the ever-popular windmill. To add drama, hazards were designed to look difficult even though easy to play. "Funnelled" cups came into use and were sometimes installed on the first few holes to give players an encouraging start.

The schism widened between owners whose goal was to provide fun in a colorful and picturesque setting and those dedicated to demitasse golf as a serious and lasting competitive sport. Don Clayton, founder of Putt-Putt® Golf and Games, has been the most vocal advocate of miniature golf as a serious sport. Disgusted by what he considered to be trick shots, in 1953 he designed a new and improved course that allowed only straight putting with none of the gimmicks. Along with McDonald's and Holiday Inn, Putt-Putt® went on to become one of the nation's first franchised roadside businesses. Many may think miniature

Plans for basement and backyard courses were popular in the early postwar years. Articles cheerfully suggested ways in which the junk accumulated in suburban garages and attics could be easily and cheaply transformed into hazards. *Popular Mechanics,* **June 1950.**

74

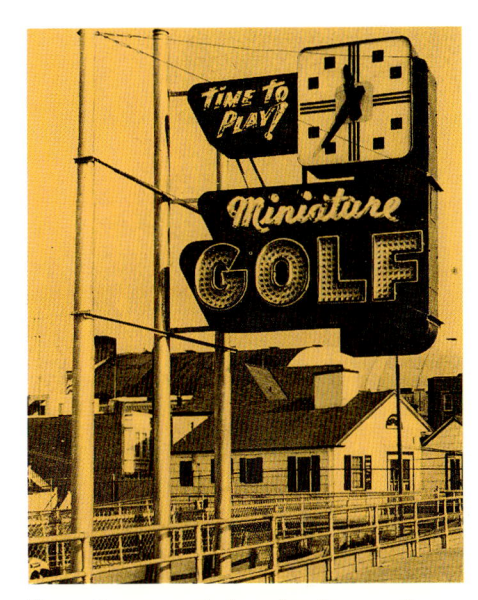

These "exaggerated modern" neon signs illustrate the necessity for miniature golf to compete with other stripside attractions. *Golf Operators Handbook*, National Golf Foundation, 1956.

golf is unlikely to be widely regarded as a sport, but who could better praise its virtues than Clayton: "Our putters are great athletes and great men. We have made competition out of a thing that was recreational. I believe this is the type of drive and commerce that made this country great." The Puritan play ethic rises again.

Lomma Enterprises of Scranton, Pennsylvania, founded in 1955 by Al Lomma, is another independent course operator. Seeking to "revolutionize the game of miniature golf," Lomma led in the revival of wacky, animated, trick hazards. Intended to be more challenging than straight putting, these hazards required both accurately aimed shots

Route 1 Miniature Golf, Saugus, Massachusetts

75

and split-second timing to avoid spinning windmill blades, revolving statuary, and other careening obstacles.

At the same time, homemade miniature golf courses became popular with hobbyists. Magazines such as *Popular Mechanics*, which catered to the do-it-yourselfer, ran articles instructing ambitious daddies on how to construct rec-room links in the finished basements of newly erected suburban tract houses. That they seemed to bear a faint resemblance to bomb shelters — another popular do-it-yourself project of the time — is not really surprising. What better way to spend one's days waiting for the smoke to clear and the fallout to blow over!

Nag's Head, North Carolina

Panama City Beach, Florida

A unique theme-course showing unauthorized use of artillery and cast-off war matériel on this unidentified military base. *Golf Operators Handbook*, National Golf Foundation, 1956.

The Gate of Paradise in the form of an oversize pay phone. Simply made of plywood, nails, and paint, hazards of the fifties usually were made by the course owners themselves. *Golf Operators Handbook*, National Golf Foundation, 1956.

A second generation of putters on a Canadaigua Lake, New York, course. By this time real windmills and lighthouses had become vanishing artifacts. COURTESY AUTHORS

Playing Miniature Golf, Roseland Park on Canandaigua Lake, New York

77

Jockey's Ridge Miniature Golf, Nags Head, North Carolina

The age of the atom bomb saw American youth fascinated with Godzilla, Mothra, dinosaurs, volcanoes, and other disruptive icons. They became the stars of both movies and miniature golf courses.

Golden Dragon Golf, North Myrtle Beach, South Carolina

78

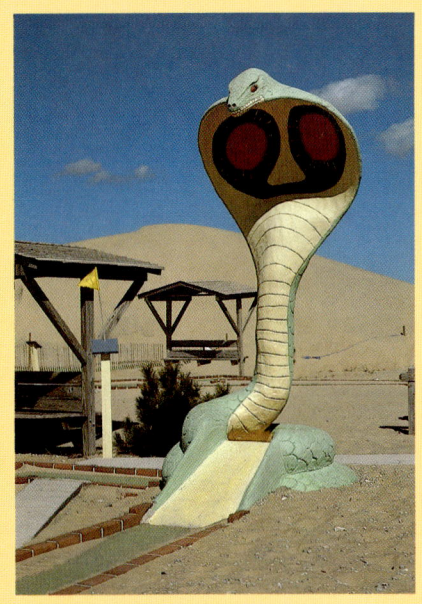

**Jockey's Ridge Miniature Golf,
Nags Head, North Carolina**

**Sir Goony Golf,
Chattanooga, Tennessee**

(*Right*) **Goofy Golf,
Panama City**

Holiday Golf, Daytona Shores, Florida

Route 1 Miniature Golf, Saugus, Massachusetts

Jekyll Island Miniature Golf, Jekyll Island, Georgia

Magic Carpet Golf, Key West, Florida

Magic Carpet Golf, Fort Walton Beach, Florida

Jawor's Fun Golf, Roseville, Michigan

(*Right*) Magic Carpet Golf, Key West, Florida

IN OUR TIME

(*Above right*) Peter Pan Miniature Golf, Austin, Texas

(*Below*) Penguin Miniature Golf, Lenox, Massachusetts

(*Bottom*) Stewart Beach Mini Golf, Galveston, Texas

In our own time miniature golf has been described as "an enduring American folk art," "the great American trash sport of the 20th century," "a map for imagined experience," and "the feeblest outdoor activity this side of waiting for a bus." No one denies that its days as "fake golf" ended long ago. It is no longer a substitute for something else. Miniature golf is miniature golf in all its loony complexity and contradiction. People play it because they love it.

Just as their parents and grandparents did nearly sixty years ago, adults, teenagers, and children can lose themselves in a silly, charming, make-believe world. For adults, it's a fairly inexpensive and relaxing way to entertain their kids — and themselves, too; for teenagers it's a cheap, fun date; and for children, it's the time of their lives when they actually get to visit cartoonland. However, instead of strolling over to the local corner-lot course, families and teenagers hop on the freeway, or go down to the resort strip, or over to the main commercial drag to get to their favorite course. In much of late-20th-century America, the vacant corner lot is a rarity, and it's only out near the roaring expressway or a locale similarly unfit for peaceful human habitation that miniature golf courses flourish.

Elaborate four-color brochures styled on highly romantic tourist literature, video arcades, waterslides, and go-carts have all been added to the course owner's arsenal to keep 'em coming back to artificial turf and sprayed cement rockeries. Judging by the fact that movie theaters seem to be shrinking to the size of screening rooms while miniature golf courses seem to be taking on Disneyland-esque proportions, it would appear that peewee golf, which seemed to have lost every battle, has perhaps won the war with filmdom.

Since the early days of the game, there has been a stylistic divergence between the courses of the East and West coasts. Southern California chains, such as Castle Park and Golf 'n' Stuff, undoubtedly influenced by Hollywood, are more elaborate, draw more heavily on fantasy, and sometimes approach the grandiosity of motion picture back-lots. The courses are intricate sets upon which every player can be the star of his own private movie. Architect Charles Moore has called miniature golf "one of Southern California's true art forms."

In contrast, East Coast courses have always been less theatrical and smaller, due to a shorter season and harsher weather. Many East Coast courses, particularly in the Northeast, have literary or historical themes. The Northeast also seems to be a haven for the funkier folk artists of miniature golf. Among these is T. J. Neil, whose "World of Concrete Sculpture" tourist attraction was until recently located in Wentworth, New Hampshire. Neil is the artist responsible for creating Patsy the Whale and other unforgettable creatures. His statues have a lovely, soft, handmade feel—no mean trick when working with such coarse materials as concrete and chicken wire.

As we move south, the "Myrtle Beach Style," named for its origin, is characterized

Animals on miniature golf courses are a relatively recent innovation and run the gamut from realistic to stylized, sometimes inhabiting elaborate artificial environments. Ingeniously, the hilly landscapes of jungle courses are often made of fill saved from digging the dyed-blue-water hazards. At Fairway Golf, St. Paul, Minnesota, fiberglass farm animals seem to migrate blindly toward a clubhouse designed to resemble a barn.

**Gorilla Country Golf,
Atlantic Beach, North Carolina**

**Bamboo Golf,
Ocean City, Maryland**

Elephant graveyard, Old Pro Golf, Ocean City, Maryland

by large central rockeries made of sprayed synthetic rock over which water, dyed blue or gold, cascades dramatically into an artificial pond whose color also has been enhanced. Invariably a jungle atmosphere is invoked, replete with palm trees, thatched huts, and fiberglass "wild" animals. The style can be seen along the Eastern Seaboard from Myrtle Beach on down.

Another East Coast tradition is embodied in the Goofy Golf courses based in Panama City Beach, Florida. They have been given their form in large part by Lee Koplin, who one night had a nightmare in which he was pursued by a host of terrifying creatures. Soon after, he became inspired to jazz up the old windmills and other run-of-the-mill gimmicks by erecting new ones in the form of giant monsters.

Mauro's Miniature Golf, Hazel Park, Michigan

A gallery of characters created by the inimitable T.J. Neil: Patsy the Whale, Ali Gator, and Princess Tina.

(*Above*) West Main Mini Golf, Hyannis Port, Massachusetts

(*Right*) Putter's Paradise West Yarmouth, Massachusetts

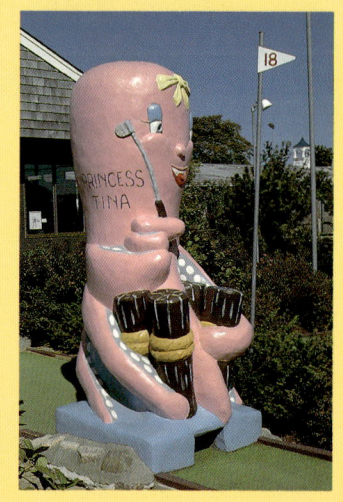

Wire mesh, fiberglass, and a lot of imagination can go a long way in the hands of some miniature golf master-builders. Sir Goony Golf, Chattanooga, Tennessee

Sir Goony Golf's Donna Davis applies the finishing touches. Chattanooga, Tennessee.

Magic Carpet Golf, Fort Walton Beach, Florida

87

WINDMILLS OF THE MIND

An example of how deeply miniature golf has penetrated American consciousness is reflected in the work of a number of contemporary artists inspired by the camp, goofy, quintessentially American qualities of minigolf. Steve Gianakos designed a course for an estate on Long Island whose hazards, like his drawings and paintings, skirt the bounds of good taste. Bill and Mary Buchen designed a room-sized sculpture in the form of a miniature golf course that produced melodic sounds when played. Rodney Alan Greenblat, who long harbored a dream to design a full eighteen-hole golf course, in 1985 (along with other New York City artists) created hazards for an indoor course erected for one evening in the trendy nightclub Palladium. His colorful, elaborately embellished bridge bore the aphorism: "Miniature Golf Is a Metaphor for Your Life."

Europe may have its centuries-old traditions of landscape architecture, but America has miniature golf. All miniature golf courses contain what J.B. Jackson described in *The Necessity for Ruins* as the essential elements of a garden: dwelling, road, shrine, and landscape. Similarly, elaborate rockeries, waterfalls, and man-made ponds have been a part of the links for over fifty years. Ornate Renaissance gardens often incorporated grottoes and waterfalls, and statues of imaginary beasts and gods were enshrined in niches and on pedestals as "reminders of ancestral beliefs." From the very beginning Garnet and

(**Opposite above**) Putters go ape! in this 1983 drawing by Steve Gianakos. Fay Wray, where are you now? COLLECTION OF MARTIN MARGULIES, COURTESY BARBARA TOLL FINE ART, INC., NEW YORK CITY

This elaborate bridge designed by Rodney Alan Greenblat first appeared at the trendy Palladium nightclub. The "Palladium Open" featured hazards by a number of New York City artists. COURTESY GRACIE MANSION GALLERY, NEW YORK CITY

(**Opposite below**) A sophisticated acoustic sculpture takes the form of an indoor course by New York artists Bill and Mary Buchen. Properly placed putts reward players with a medley of tones. COURTESY BILL AND MARY BUCHEN

88

Frieda Carter peopled their Lookout Mountain course with storybook characters and fairytale creatures. It is not too much of a leap to see that Wacky Man, Patsy the Whale, and the Mad Hatter, as well as a host of other characters, have taken the place of Venus and Mars, Apollo and Diana, as icons of the collective conscious. As the putter and putteress swing along the fairway they can view the changing panorama of tiny churches, haunted houses, mosques, and townscapes, all with parallels in the architectural follies of 18th-century Europe. These pleasure gardens evoked an atmosphere of exotic romance and fantasy. And so does miniature golf, as we hope it always will. For miniature golf, a truly indigenous American art form, is the stuff of our collective dreams.

A visitor from another land might mistake some miniature golf courses for the goal of a pilgrimage rather than a playground. Fulfilling a human need for a touch of the mystical, sphinxes and Buddhas seem at home on the links coast to coast.

Wacky Golf, North Myrtle Beach, South Carolina

Wacky Golf, Myrtle Beach, South Carolina

Magic Carpet Golf, Fort Walton Beach, Florida

90

Goofy Golf, Panama City Beach, Florida

Wacky Golf, Myrtle Beach, South Carolina

THIS REPLICA OF "THE GREAT SPHINX" IS NOT YET COMPLETED – THE BACK 14 FEET IS UNDER CONSTRUCTION AT OUR "WACKY FACTORY" in WINDY HILL

Magic Carpet Golf, Fort Walton Beach, Florida

91

(*Left*) **Sir Goony Golf, Chattanooga, Tennessee**

(*Below*) **Peter Pan Miniature Golf, Austin, Texas**

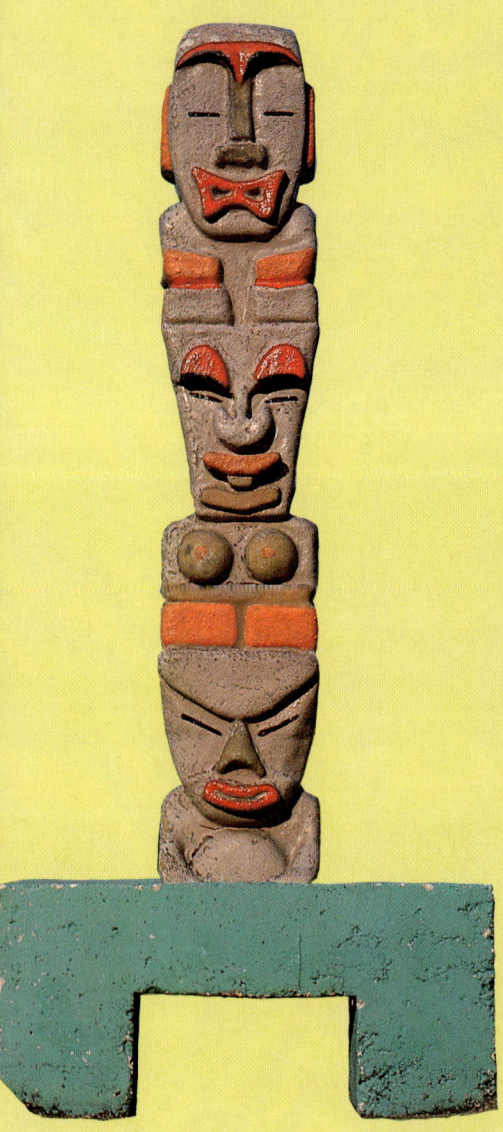

(*Above left*) Wacky Golf,
North Myrtle Beach, South Carolina

(*Above right*) Magic Carpet Golf,
Key West, Florida

(*Right*) Storybook Land Golf,
San Diego, California

93

Acknowledgments

Special thanks to: Walton Rawls of Abbeville Press for falling for the idea of this book and for being an excellent editor; Helene Silverman for her fine book design; Karal Ann Marling, Herb Schoellkopf and Rob Silberman for sharing their research materials; the miniature golf course proprietors for their kindness in allowing me to photograph and publish pictures of their businesses; Billy Adler, Susan Butler, Joseph S. Clark, Jr., Cindy Cole, Asher Edelman, Anne Edelstein, Howard Gilman, Agnes Gund, Ellen Harris, Barbara Jakobson, Philip Johnson, Carl Lobell, Dutch Magrath, Jr., Ethel Margolies, Carolyn Marsh, Jim McClure, Harold Ramis, Stephen Resnick, Ross and Judy Rosenberg, Robin Silverman, Jonathan Smith, and Erica Stoller for their moral and financial support; and the Architectural League, New York, the John Simon Guggenheim Memorial Foundation, the Design Arts and Visual Arts Programs of the National Endowment for the Arts, and the New York Foundation for the Arts for sponsoring and funding my automotive research.

Our expedition into the annals of miniature golf history would have been far more roundabout without the help of the following individuals: Charles Garfinkel, Larry Lawrence, Joseph S.F. Murdock, president of the Golf Collectors Society, Mark Rose, who generously shared his wonderful collection of midget golf memorabilia, Mrs. Bryant of the Ralph Miller Memorial Golf Library, Los Angeles; William Chapin, Edward Chapin III, and especially Barbara Massey, all of Beautiful Rock City Gardens, Harry Eckhoff of the National Golf Foundation, and Mark Soppeland.

We would also like to thank Steven Notis, James Sheppard, Rose Reidelbach, Dorothy Reidelbach, Michael Bliss, Daisy and Sam Gattengo, Chuck Hammer, Barbara Hertel, Jean Houch, Steve Hudson of SoHo Service, Anne Karanfilian, Walter Lehrman, Jayme Olitsky, Allan Schwartzman, Larry Shopmaker and Barry Skidelsky. We would like to acknowledge the work of Chester Liebs, Phil Patton, Robert Venturi, and Fernand Braudel. Lastly, many thanks to the librarians of the New York Public Library and the Cleveland Public Library whose expertise and enthusiasm made long hours of research an adventure.

Old Pro Golf, Rehoboth Beach, Delaware

Hazel Park, Michigan

Myrtle Beach, South Carolina

Pigeon Forge, Tennessee

Sea View Golf, Rehoboth Beach, Delaware

Wacky Golf, Jacksonville Beach, Florida